The Complete Guide to
Online Investing

Everything You Need to Know Explained Simply

By Michelle Hooper

The Complete Guide to Online Investing: Everything You Need to Know Explained Simply

Copyright © 2008 by Atlantic Publishing Group, Inc.
1405 SW 6th Ave. • Ocala, Florida 34471 • 800-814-1132 • 352-622-1875–Fax
Web site: www.atlantic-pub.com • E-mail: sales@atlantic-pub.com
SAN Number: 268-1250

ISBN-13: 978-1-60138-211-5   ISBN-10: 1-60138-211-1

Library of Congress Cataloging-in-Publication Data

Hooper, Michelle Dawn.
  The complete guide to online investing : everything you need to know explained simply / by Michelle Dawn Hooper.
      p. cm.
  Includes bibliographical references and index.
  ISBN-13: 978-1-60138-211-5 (alk. paper)
  ISBN-10: 1-60138-211-1 (alk. paper)
  1. Electronic trading of securities. I. Title.

  HG4515.95.H66 2008
  332.64'20285--dc22
                              2008015428

INTERIOR LAYOUT DESIGN: Nicole Deck ndeck@atlantic-pub.com

Printed on Recycled Paper

Printed in the United States

We recently lost our beloved pet "Bear," who was not only our best and dearest friend but also the "Vice President of Sunshine" here at Atlantic Publishing. He did not receive a salary but worked tirelessly 24 hours a day to please his parents. Bear was a rescue dog that turned around and showered myself, my wife Sherri, his grandparents Jean, Bob and Nancy and every person and animal he met (maybe not rabbits) with friendship and love. He made a lot of people smile every day.

We wanted you to know that a portion of the profits of this book will be donated to The Humane Society of the United States.

–Douglas & Sherri Brown

THE HUMANE SOCIETY
OF THE UNITED STATES.©

The human-animal bond is as old as human history. We cherish our animal companions for their unconditional affection and acceptance. We feel a thrill when we glimpse wild creatures in their natural habitat or in our own backyard.

Unfortunately, the human-animal bond has at times been weakened. Humans have exploited some animal species to the point of extinction.

The Humane Society of the United States makes a difference in the lives of animals here at home and worldwide. The HSUS is dedicated to creating a world where our relationship with animals is guided by compassion. We seek a truly humane society in which animals are respected for their intrinsic value, and where the human-animal bond is strong.

Want to help animals? We have plenty of suggestions. Adopt a pet from a local shelter, join The Humane Society and be a part of our work to help companion animals and wildlife. You will be funding our educational, legislative, investigative and outreach projects in the U.S. and across the globe.

Or perhaps you'd like to make a memorial donation in honor of a pet, friend or relative? You can through our Kindred Spirits program. And if you'd like to contribute in a more structured way, our Planned Giving Office has suggestions about estate planning, annuities, and even gifts of stock that avoid capital gains taxes.

Maybe you have land that you would like to preserve as a lasting habitat for wildlife. Our Wildlife Land Trust can help you. Perhaps the land you want to share is a backyard—that's enough. Our Urban Wildlife Sanctuary Program will show you how to create a habitat for your wild neighbors.

So you see, it's easy to help animals. And The HSUS is here to help.

The Humane Society of the United States
2100 L Street NW
Washington, DC 20037
202-452-1100
www.hsus.org

Table of Contents

Chapter 6: The Safety of Online Investing 195

Chapter 7: Brokers and Financial Advisors   203

Chapter 8: Finding Your Investment Style   219

Chapter 9: Chart Matters   233

Chapter 10: Taxes   249

Chapter 11: Random Thoughts   265

Introduction

O ver 20 years ago, the Internet began to take over many aspects of what is now called the "old school" way of doing things. Computers can be used for a wide variety of tasks, and it is rare for an individual not to own a computer. Those individuals who wish to plan for their future can use computers to calculate how much a certain investment at a certain percentage for so many years contributes to a comfortable lifestyle. The Internet adds convenience to the calculation, because calling a broker to help with this information can be time-consuming.

Some believe military computers began the use of the Internet in the late 1960s, but that was a failure, as it turned out to be essentially a scientific research project not meant for the massive, worldwide transfer of information available today. In its earliest incarnations it was just designated for military use. It was during this time that electronic mail, packet switching (traveling information), and transport control protocol (exchanging the packets) were discovered, but the ideas were not fully supported. This left nearly a decade before the Internet saw public use in the 1980s and became a huge part of pop culture, particularly on the West Coast. By the early 1990s, the phenomenon was the most prevalent home addition. Technology is said to take away business from many, including personal financial firms and advisors. Staying afloat on the trends of the Internet helps all because it is an excellent marketing tool. Because the Internet is an everyday tool for nearly everyone, people have become thoroughly educated with the Internet, and some cannot leave home without it. Blackberries and cell phones are becoming so technologically advanced and new tools are being invented every day to keep up with the growing trend. Internet sources are available everywhere. Just when you think it cannot get any better, who knows what inventors will think of next.

Many investors have the knowledge they need already to make investments, but there are times when you are just not sure what to do and when to do it. This is when the investment brokers come in. Stock markets can crash one day and be right back where they were the next day. There is no trickery involved here, it is just the way it is, and there is nothing anyone can do about it. Investors have to be educated and resourceful when making investments, although many seem to follow the trends, which is not always the best thing to do. Investors get scared and pull out of stocks when they drop, frightened they will lose all their money. In some respects, this is a good decision – unless that stock skyrockets the next day.

There are beginning investors and mainstream investors. Beginners should start out small, and with time, more money, and education, work to develop an investment portfolio that brings desirable returns while seeing excellent cash flows. The cash flow is the progress of a stock company where the actual cash that flows through is measured during a specific period. In reviewing a company's income statement, depreciations are deducted in addition to other expenses, resulting in determining the net income of a company. Beforehand though, that total number is the actual cash flow. Rate of returns is what you expect from your investment before taxes. Mainstream investors are the higher-net individuals who are not afraid to lose $20,000 or so. Really though, no one wants to lose anything. Investing is easy, but it is not meant for everyone. If you get mad at casinos, then you should probably hire a broker. Stock markets offer a variety of sources, such as the National Association of Securities Dealers Automated and Quotations, the American Stock and Options Exchange, Dow Jones and more, each of which is updated regularly as the times and the numbers, they are a-changin'. No doubt, the market is a whirlwind of information; you have a lot to learn. This book is written to educate an investor making the first foray into the Internet investment world without becoming boring. The chapters will describe different types of stock investments, mutual fund options, how to invest, and what you should or should not do. The book will provide up-to-date graphics and charts to learn the basics in a simple manner. Web sites will be mentioned as well.

"Money is better than poverty, if only for financial reasons."-
Woody Allen

Acknowledgments

A significant part of this book was written at night and seldom did I have much time on the weekends to get much of anything done. My social life disappeared for a while and often times, I hid the phone. Some days, I was no where to be found. My mother (Judy Fisher) often called to see if I was still alive.

This book is being completed in the winter months of 2007 in northern California. There has not been much rain, nor is there any snow while the eastern states have been hit by winter storms. I sit here in peace with the bedroom door shut and the blinds down trying to eliminate even the least bit of noise. My cat is staring at me for no reason. She is cross-eyed. On this particular day, it is overcast outside, but I look at the bright side, Christmas is coming in a week. My every intention in writing this book is to educate both first-time investors and those full-fledged who are always willing to learn something new. I take pride in this investment story, for it is an accomplishment and it was not easy. It has been fun and challenging and I hope the readers' enjoy it. I warn you my sense of humor, it is dry.

A special thanks to my editor Angela C. Adams for giving me this opportunity as well as the other editors at Atlantic Publishing for their wonderful sense of editing. I'm a writer and thank someone of a higher power for "good" editors. I thank you all for believing in me. I am also grateful to those whom I interviewed for the case studies throughout the book. Your advice helped me paint a prettier picture. My brother, Jeff Sherman, is special to me with his mad photography skills. In the bright Fresno sunlight, he worked diligently and patiently to capture a photo of me with my eyes open. My payback to my avoided friends is such that you should read every line as you are probably mentioned somewhere somehow throughout the book. In a land of euphoria, either you've lost some money, are financially loaded, or you are set for retirement. You can thank me or yell at me later, but keep in mind I was thinking of you.

Positivism is the key and I surround myself in those environments. That said, I would also like to thank my writing professor Laurena Mayne Davis, for teaching me a few things. I hope that I have taught you something, too. And to my friend Sandra D. Davis, for pushing me to go on with perseverance, even when I did not feel like it. I have come a long way and intend to go further. Good things will come.

Scatterbrained she wrote, but the job got done and the full package lies in your hands. To you from me; enjoy. It is going to be a while before I write another book.

I dedicate this book to my grandmother Josefita Gallegos. You are missed.

CHAPTER 1

What is Investing?

Simply put, stocks are shares of a particular company that are traded on the market both privately and publicly, while bonds are over-the-counter (OTC) commodities. Bonds are not on a formal exchange, which makes them OTC at all times. Some stock is OTC because it does not meet the regulations required to be on a more centralized exchange; this includes stock in smaller companies unable to meet listing requirements. Stocks of this nature are exchanged on an over-the-counter-bulletin-board at **http://www.otcbb.com**.

IMPORTANT KEY TERMS

(1) **Dividends** are the key, as they pay shareholders profits earned from an investment. However, there is

no obligation for any company to do so. The portion of a company's earnings paid back to an investor is usually viewed as a good thing. Dividends are referred to as a dollar amount per share. These dividends do not have to be reinvested and can be cashed out at anytime. Senior investors may use these dividends as part of retirement incomes when there is a fixed amount involved because they are stable. Because the stock market can be questionable at times, dividends feel like an accomplishment to those investors who are involved through a bouncing economy. Dividends are positive in any case because they enhance a stocks total return in addition to outpacing inflation. Reinvesting the dividends simply multiplies stock shares.

(2) **Capital appreciation**, which is a hoped-for increase from your share purchase price to the actual market price.

(3) A **security** is represented as a certificate or an electronic book entry while derivatives are instruments that reduce risk between parties offering a nice return on an investment. This is meant to help an investor in both the timing and payoff of an investment. In addition, a derivative can include stocks and bonds interest rates, exchange rates, and inflation conditions.

(4) **Bonds** are noted for the debt or fixed-income market, meaning participants can buy or sell, but at a bigger risk because of the lack of liquidity (converting stock into cash). Most investors include bigger institutions like banks, pension funds, and mutual funds.

HISTORY CONTINUES

SECURITIES ACT OF 1933

This act is also known as the "truth in securities" law. This law requires that financial, management, and other important information about public sale securities be given to investors. The law was also passed to keep the sale of securities from being fraudulent, deceitful, or misrepresented. This law defines security as any "note, stock, treasury stock, security future, bond, debenture, evidence of indebtedness, certificate of interest or participation in any profit-sharing agreement, collateral-trust certificate, organization certificate or subscription, transferable share, investment contract, voting-trust certificate, certificate of deposit for a security, fractional undivided interest in oil, gas, or other mineral rights, any put, call, straddle, option or privilege on any security, certificate of deposit, or group or index of securities (including any interest therein)." It also refers to foreign currency regarding "put, call, straddle, option, or privilege." **http://www.sec.gov/about/laws/sa33.pdf**

SECURITIES EXCHANGE ACT OF 1934

This act by Congress created the Securities and Exchange Commission (SEC), which has authority over the securities industry. It can oversee, regulate, and register clearing agencies, brokerage firms, transfer agents, and SROs. The New York Stock Exchange, the National Association of Securities Dealers (NASDAQ) and the American Stock Exchange are SROs. It gives the commission power to discipline regulated entities if the need arises as certain types of market conduct are not condoned. The SEC may require publicly traded companies to report periodic information.

MALONEY ACT OF 1938

This act provided for the supervision of over-the-counter securities market. It also called for reorganization of the New York Stock Exchanges and amended the 1934 Securities Exchange Act. The OTC investor is protected under this act the same as with the national securities exchanges.

TRUST INDENTURE ACT OF 1939

Bonds, debentures, or notes, known as debt securities, that are for sale to the public are regulated by this act. The issuer of the bond and the bondholder must have a formal agreement conforming to this act's standards.

INVESTMENT ADVISORS ACT OF 1940

Individual advisers or firms dealing in advice for compensation must register with the SEC. They also have to conform to regulations that offer protection to investors. This Act, amended in 1996, now usually requires only advisors with $25 million under management to register.

INVESTMENT COMPANY ACT OF 1940

Companies that deal mainly in investing, trading securities, and reinvesting and offer their own stock for sale are governed by this act. They must let investors know their investment policies and financial condition upon original sale and then on a regular basis.

SECURITIES INVESTOR PROTECTION ACT OF 1970

This act established the Securities Investor Protection Corporation (SIPC) to protect investors from a failed brokerage firm. If cash and/or securities are missing from an account most investors are able to get their money back through SIPC. There are some losses not covered, such as falling values. Instead, missing securities are replaced. Investors who are sold worthless securities are not covered by SIPC.

SECURITIES ACT AMENDMENTS OF 1975

This law amends the Securities Exchange Act of 1934. The SEC is directed to help establish a National Market System. New regulations were introduced regarding securities handling. Clearing agencies are required to register with the SEC. National Market System is a trading system for OTC sponsored by NASDAQ and NASD. It also is a trading system for the NYSE to list prices for stocks and bonds.

INSIDER TRADING SANCTIONS ACT OF 1984

This act increases penalties for insider information that is used to gain profit. The SEC can issue fines up to triple the profits or avoided losses that insiders get using nonpublic information.

INSIDER TRADING ACT OF 1988

This act is designed to punish insider trading and may pay money to persons providing information about insider trading.

SARBANES-OXLEY ACT OF 2002

This act created the "Public Company Accounting Oversight Board" (PCAOB). Their responsibility is to make sure the auditing profession does not engage in fraud. Corporate responsibility and financial disclosures are mandated by reforms in this Act.

Life with the government may not always be the greatest adventure. Cappy began working for the Department of Treasury in 1980. In 1986, the government proposed a Thrift Savings Plan, similar to a 401K. Having never invested in this sort of plan, Cappy didn't know where to begin or what to research. The government had given her five options to choose from for his long-term plan. While many of her colleagues pursued outside help with brokerage firms, Cappy sought the advice of a benefits counselor in the office. But what Cappy didn't know is that those who received the advice from a broker knew that as an investor, you had to stay up-to-date more often than not on the stock and bonds markets. She had not been counseled enough to know that he could shift her earnings. In 2003, her stock plummeted after 9/11 happened and the war in Iraq began. Cappy lost quite a bit of money after this, but he recovered it quickly enough and reallocated what was left. The economy was a mess at this point. This explains how quickly investors can be affected and why it is important to learn as much as possible as a first-time investor.

INITIAL PUBLIC OFFERINGS (IPOS)

IPOs consist of shares of publicly-traded companies, offered to first-time investors. In a way, IPOs are like real estate, as there is more demand than supply in many cases.

"Historically, IPOs have been an investment opportunity offered mostly to favored clients of participating brokerage firms, investment bankers, and venture capitalists." (Price, 177). These folks choose from the best of the best, while the rest of the population only chooses from the leftovers. These days though, those leftovers can be just as good. During trading, prices rise quickly, and they are sometimes difficult to get into. An IPO takes place when a private company has its first sale of stock to the public. The stock can either be available from a smaller company or a larger, privately owned company looking to become public. A stock will go public for expansion or research purposes. During this process, the company will lose full control of everything once it goes public, and liability will increase because shareholders can sue for any misinformation. However, there are more pros than cons, and even mergers or acquisitions are a hot commodity because a smaller company can easily be purchased by those larger ones.

The investor must be careful, as IPOs are simply transition periods that have an uncertain future. A track record of a new company proceeding to expand is not available. The typical buyer is an institutional investor, such as pension funds, college endowments, insurance companies, and high net-worth individuals. This type of investment is risky. The companies have every intention of raising extra capital for their shares on the public exchange network, because large volumes of stock assume a role of a nice opportunity for future establishment and growth. The difference is that the company does not have to negotiate with individual investors; it just has to raise money through the larger market, which seems to be more appealing.

Like any other stock, the research should always be done. Even the management of the company accounts for something. Be wary about the underwriters. Underwriters are the people that assist in taking a company public, and a better underwriter means a better and stronger company. With the best underwriters, you are assured that the company has an excellent research department and excellent resources. Within a company's prospectus from the SEC, you should find these underwriters within the first couple of pages. Examples of underwriting companies include *Bank of America Securities, Bear Stearns, Blackstone Group LP, Chase H&Q, Credit Suisse First Boston, Deutsche Bank AG, First Data Corp., Goldman Sach's, Gruntal & Co, J.P. Morgan, Lehman Brothers, Merrill Lynch, Morgan Stanley Dean Witter, Robertson Stephens, and Thomas Weisel Partners*. It is best to go with the most reputable underwriters such as Merrill Lynch, as they have the best reputations and can provide some peace of mind.

PRIVATE COMPANIES VERSUS PUBLIC COMPANIES

A private company is attractive to some investors because the financial information is kept secret. While it still possesses shares and holders, a private company lacks what is called a 10-K, which permits a comprehensive annual report of a company to be viewed by all under the Security and Exchange Commission. Competitors are unable to see what is really going in private companies. Other advantages include skimming the surface of government regulations that a public offering would need to abide by, such as certain quarterly profit sale or margins.

A private company may choose to go public because a growth for more capital business is desired. It allows the company to pay off debt quicker while increasing exposure for the company. While founding investors may be looking to sell off part of their ownership, the company may also be looking to recruit upper management. Those who usually purchase IPOs have deeper pockets buying shares under value, but quickly selling them too. Public companies issue stock either OTC or through the stock exchange through an IPO. Documents must be filed through the Security Exchange Commission, making every financial statement available. This includes sales literature in which the investment is presented, annual reports, audited financial statements, and a prospectus.

Some people may turn their nose to the privately held companies, but there are some well-known folks in the mix, including Pricewaterhouse Coopers, Publix Super Markets, Koch Industries, and Hallmark Cards. The United States Postal Service just went on the public stock exchange within the past few years, while Domino's Pizza joined the public in 2007. IKEA is likeable company; the furniture store is a privately held stock. Good references to start with are determining whether your interest is public or private include Mergent Online (once Moody's), Hoover's Online, and Lexis-Nexis. The most suitable Web source would be the Security Exchange Commission.

INITIAL PUBLIC OFFERINGS WEB SITES

Alert-IPO
www.ostman.com/alert-ipo

CatchIPO
www.catchipo.com

FreeEDGAR
www.freeedgar.com

IPO Central
www.ipocentral.com

IPO Data Systems
www.ipodata.com

IPO Intelligence Online
www.ipo-fund.com

IPO Maven
www.ipomaven.com

IPO Monitor
www.ipomonitor.com

Multrex Investor Network
www.multrexinvestor.com

Primark
www.primark.com

Quote.com
www.quote.com

SECURITY EXCHANGE COMMISSION

These folks protect you, the investor, from the scandalous people that are out to get your money. The commission provides economic growth and sound market regulation. Much of the enforcement action is caused from concerns of the investors themselves, and every year hundreds of individuals and companies violate this law. The main service the SEC provides the investors is a regulation that forces federal government, stocks, bonds, and more to provide you with the necessary information before you make an investment. This does not prevent you from losing your money, as you never know what is going to happen, but the finances and background information seem like a logical consideration. One amenity of the SEC is that its Web site (**www.sec.gov**) can provide you with complaints about a particular company. As much as you would like to think otherwise, not everything on the Internet is true. The SEC will continue to do its best on pinpointing investment scams. Filed complaints through the SEC are available at all times, and the most common include major stock price fluctuations, not disclosing information, misrepresenting facts, market manipulation, and unfairness. Regarding disputes among brokers and shareholders, the most favored way to go is through an arbitration hearing, keeping the courts out of it. It is less costly although attorneys can be present. Verdicts are resolved via contract and sufficient evidence, otherwise litigation will take place. Litigation can be costly, and it is usually based on large monetary damages. You could end up spending more than you lost, so you have to weigh the options to determine if it is worth it.

In days of yore, requesting a document was a long process because everything had to be mailed, one at a time. Disclosure forms were once filed by paper in Washington, and when anyone needed a document it was important to know exactly which one before it was mailed. There were tons of documents that had to be sorted through just for one request. Since 1996, companies are required to provide as much information as possible on EDGAR on any trade exchange condition. Reports must be filed within the 90 days before ending the fiscal year; therefore, those companies whose fiscal year ends December 31 have a deadline in April the following year.

In other matters, The National Association of Securities Dealers also helps prevent fraud; to be explained in the next chapter.

ELECTRONIC DATA GATHERING, ANALYSIS, AND RETRIEVAL SYSTEM

www.edgar-online.com

This is the SECs database, in which financial information is made available to the public. It is a search engine, and you can research a business by name, location, filing, date, and ticker symbol. This is actually the first step in doing research on a stock company that has caught your eye. When referring to financial information, you can retrieve a prospectus, which shows its security offerings. A proxy solicitation document is also available on this site for those shareholders who can vote. Reports are always filed on any kind of corporate changes, such as IPO filings, but the most important are the annual report, which discloses just about everything.

Most companies voluntarily submit their annual reports to EDGAR, but reports of the 10-K or 10-KSB are mandatory. With the 10-K, a company must offer a comprehensive review of business dealings through the year and the 10-KSB, small business reports. A company has 60 days after the end of its fiscal year (FY) to file these reports. If you already own stock in a company, then that stock is required to mail a physical or electronic copy of that stock at the end of the FY. Even as a potential investor you will learn if there are any serious litigations, but one rule of thumb is to note that it is quite normal for a company to be facing several lawsuits. You will also learn of recent developments, and the competition that is involved. Aside from financial statements, you will be able to review what the future plans are for the company, despite any negative retractions. Quarterly reports are also available, known as 10-Qs. With a 10-KSB, the report is not as comprehensive. This report can be filed within 90 days after the fiscal year.

There is an EDGAR online Web site, in which all company data is organized in a presentable and fashionable way, making it easier for investors to find background information on broker individuals and companies. Users must register and not everything is free, but it is convenient. In contrast, there is a Web site called FreeEDGAR in which the investor can compile as much information as desired on the condition that it is available. Everything is fully indexed as it becomes available. **www.freeedgar.com**. With the type of a ticker symbol, you can retrieve filings from the past three years.

ABOUT THOSE STOCKS...

If you like to shop, do not worry because this market has a lot to offer. If you do not like to shop, hire a broker. You have a few options below. The value of a stock is determined by underlying economical factors. It is the present value of future dividends, and it is an analyst's job to project what this will be; dividends are based on the company profit. You can distinguish among bonds by growth size, company size, and sectors. Stocks tend to be well ahead of inflation, bonds, and other investment vehicles when it comes to your desired returns, making them the best pool for long-term investing. What it costs going into a stock does not tell you what its earning potential is, therefore, any given amount may seem cheap going in, but it depends on the company, earning prospects, or lack thereof. In learning whether a stock is overvalued or undervalued, you simply look at the revenue, cash flow, earnings, and other tracings. The market capitalization of a stock determines its size, while the share price equals the total number of shares outstanding (stock currently held by investors) based on what investors think its value is.

Aside from stocks, commodity futures are a class of their own. They still offer diversification for a portfolio except there are not nearly as many things to choose from as there are in stocks. There are about 40 commodities to choose from, including things given by the natural earth such as gold, silver, corn, oil, and livestock. Even real estate and collectibles fit in somewhere. This is for the investors who have much more money to risk, if they invest as folks in the industry believe you will have more luck with an initial investment of at least $10,000, but the investor can allocate any amount that is wished. The investment offers large profits within a short amount of time. Similar to any investment, you can invest big with as much as you like although the risk is great. Unfortunately, risk can never be eliminated. When investing in a commodity, it is called futures because of a contract negotiation in which there is a time for your investment. Buying a futures contract is the same as betting on a stock; one hopes to go up. To minimize your losses, you can sell your commodity but you will still lose money. On the other hand, it is up to the investors on when to buy or sell. An investment in commodities offers great returns, however they have a reputation for being riskier. An energy sector is included, such as natural gas and heating oil, or even agriculture where you can you can get your coffee, corn, cotton, and soybeans. Of course, unpredictable natural disasters happen, which are another reason to invest conservatively. Metals are part of the offer with copper, aluminum, lead, nickel, and more as an industrial investment. If you are into livestock, there are pork belly buys, cattle, and more. Starbucks is a commodity, and the researchers involved spend a lot of time on economic and climatic conditions among other things before purchasing raw coffee. Brokers do not do this sort of thing, and only the experts of coffee know when to get involved. (Price, 66). Arbitrage is when you buy a commodity on one market and at the same time sell it at a higher price on another market.

Like the SEC, there is the Commodity Futures Trading Commission, which regulates the option markets in the United States. Created in 1974, agriculture led the way, followed by the rest. The commission protects investors against fraud, manipulation, and bad trading practices, while maintaining competition and efficiency. Regarding taxes, this is a positive thing; profits are taxed as 60-percent long-term capital gains and 40-percent short-term capital gains.

WEB SITES

Commodity Futures Trading Commission
www.cftc.gov

Data Broadcast Corp.
www.dbd.com

Freese-Notis Weather
www.weather.net

Futures Industry Institute
www.fiafi.org

Futures.net
www.futures.net

Futures Online
www.futuresmag.com

Futuresource.com
www.futuresource.com

Ino.com
www.ino.com

Linco Futures Group
www.lfgllc.com

National Futures Association
www.nfa.futures.org

National Weather Service
www.nws.noaa.gov

Options Industry Council
www.optionscentral.com

OptionSource

www.optionsource.com

PC Trader
www.pctrader.com

TradingCharts.com
www.tfc-charts.w2d.com

Weather Channel
www.weather.com

World Link Futures
www.worldlinkfutures.com

COMMODITIES

Without commodities, there would be no morning coffee, lumber to build homes, gas, bling-bling, and anything else we like to use daily. The gas we put in our cars is based upon the trading activity done daily which then affects the price. Commodity traders vie for a liquid market. This means there are a lot of people interested and are willing to trade. This information is important to stock traders because of the economy cycles. If an investor is deep into the Exxon stock and the earnings from the commodity "oil" are failing, this is how it affects the investor. It then affects the share prices when trades are taking place. Anytime a commodity increases it hurts that company in which the products are the main source of income, and it then can affect the company earnings.

A FEW EXAMPLES OF COMMODITY EXCHANGES	
New York Mercantile Exchange	www.nymex.com
Chicago Board of Trade	www.cbot.com
Chicago Mercantile Exchange	www.cme.com

The supply-and-demand gesture is what makes a commodity stock. During an inflationary period, revenues of stock companies tend to increase and with a demand, there is more pressure which can benefit investors. Those companies where the stock is needed such as oil tend to have stronger gains which benefit those investors of the stock market where allocations have been made. Growth companies in particular largely support this investing, and prices for a commodity are soaring. View Standard and Poor 500 on further information for stock investors. Commodities and futures are both regulated differently than stocks. While an investor may have an account for stocks and bonds through a brokerage already, that brokerage may not be able to assist with commodities and futures as a separate account would be necessary to begin trading.

Trading in commodities can be very scary and expensive. But once you are versed in basic trading techniques in the stock market, you can consider moving on to more advanced trading. There are many different methods that can be used. There are fundamental supply-and-demand information, versed technical analysis using charts or moving averages, trend-following approach or countertrend, and day trading. If you are just starting out consider testing all of the different methods and then decide what seems to fit you the best and hopefully make you the most profit. Do not be afraid to use more than one method at the same time even though they will occasionally offset each other. As the Boy Scouts say, "Be prepared" and be confident that you will be successful. Develop your trading plan, taking all the necessary steps to avoid as many pitfalls as possible. Do not have a fly-by-the-seat-of-your-pants attitude; think your plan through as completely as you can. Ask yourself how much money you have to invest realizing that the more you have the better chance you have to succeed in the long run. A lot of capital lets you be more flexible so you can adopt two or more trading plans and trade in several markets at one time. Now that you have developed your plan and know how much capital you are willing to risk you need to decide how much you will invest in each trade. Do you want to be timid or aggressive? The higher percentage per trade will give a better return but also can mean a larger loss if things do not go right. Consider starting out with 2-5 percent of your capital for each trade. The next question to answer in your mind is do you want to move in and out quickly, use a long-term trading method or stay somewhere in between. Again, the best way to decide what is best for you is to test several approaches. Develop a method for taking your profits and running. You will not always make the right decision; you may get out and find that the market you were in just keeps going up. Do not second guess yourself, take your profit, be happy you are making money and invest it again looking for more profit. Then there is the down side of knowing when to get out with the least amount of loss. Do not let a big hit ruin your day or future. Decide what percentage loss you can manage, take it, do not look back but move on to the next trade. There will be daily fluctuations in the market - some you lose, some you win - but do not count on every day being a major event in the trading world. Do not let yourself become emotional over either gains or losses, be objective because the market itself can be very emotional.

On to talking about some specifics about commodities. Exchange-traded funds (EFTs) in precious metals and oil have shares that can be traded through a stock exchange. Like mutual funds EFTs issue and redeem shares but the difference between the two is the size of share lots. Large investors can make an in-kind trade in the portfolio, such as shares of stocks traded, gold and bullion trades or do a reverse and get gold or stocks for stocks. Some of these shares can be sold into the exchange market and small investors are able to purchase them. Trading strategies have a wide margin of options. The most common are long calls; long puts; bull call, bear put and butterfly spreads. Find the one or ones you find comfortable with and become proficient in using them. A long call is simply purchasing a call option in which the investor hopes that the price of the futures market will rise. There is limited risk in a long call, however you do pay a premium. For instance, a coffee call option costs $400, coffee futures fall 50 points. If the contract value is $100 per point there is a $5000 value decline in the coffee futures contract. But, the upside is that you only lose your $400. Using our coffee example above, you pay $400, coffee futures rise 50 points. You would lose $5000 if you had sold short in the futures contract itself, but this way you only lose your $400. A strike price is the market price that the commodity " underlying a call or put option can be purchased (call) or sold (put)." If you buy a call option with a lower strike price and sell a different call option with a higher strike price with the same expiration date it is called a bull call spread. This is also a limited risk venture but also has limited profit possibilities. If you are somewhat bullish about a market this is a good venture.

In the reverse if you buy a put option with a higher strike price, sell another put option with lower strike price, with the same expiration date now you are venturing into a bear put spread. Again, this is a limited risk with limited profit. If you are somewhat bearish about a market this is a good venture. The butterfly spread (not margarine made from butterflies) is buying a call option at a strike price, finding a higher strike price and writing two calls, then going to an even higher strike price and buying a call. Reversing this procedure is a butterfly put. This is a good strategy if the market is somewhat neutral and will remain within a certain range for a while.

The Average Directional Index (ADX), developed by Welles Wilder measures the strength of the prevailing major trends. This indicator moves between 0 and 100, below 20 indicating weakness, above 40, strength. Some traders use this as a guide to trade a certain market especially those investors who use the trend following approach.

Reports can be a major factor in futures and options markets for bonds, stock indexes and currencies. The Gross Domestic Product (GDP) shows the total of all services and goods produced in the US. It can be a market mover if it is far below or far above expectations. Oil supply reports are released weekly showing distillate, crude oil and gasoline supplies. Reports on balance of trade, retail sales, industrial production and personal income can have an effect on the futures markets. The balance of trade report will probably be the most noticed. When a larger than expected trade surplus or deficit report is issued the bond and currency markets will move.

If the US is showing more imports and less exports the futures market will move. Bond markets will suffer with a strengthening economy but stock index futures will be better. A slowing economy favors bonds but not stock indexes. Popular trading instruments are the Eurodollars which are deposits held in non-US banks. They are quoted in terms of an index and the unit of movement for futures contracts are ticks. They trade on the CME four times a year. They have a fairly good return in a short time period and offer fairly low margins. Trading should take place when interest rates are likely to change. Knowing how to trade the Eurodollars gives you the ability to trade other types of interest rate futures. If you do venture into interest rate futures be sure to consider the following factors - how much do you want to risk, is the market overbought or oversold, what is the overall trend and what the background is for your trade. Currencies can be traded over the phone but you can sit in front of your computer and actively manage your trade. Do not get up and take a break or you could lose a large sum of money. Electronic trading will cost you more to trade in the spot market than it does the pros. Some foreign currency Web sites will try to tell you there is no commission, but they collect a fee that is the difference between bid and ask.

Note: The Japanese started commodity trading with rice and the Chinese are said to be involved too somewhere in the 17th century. Commodity trading began in the United States in the 19th century, but it was not until the 1970s when the fad took off with financial instruments of foreign currencies. Market conditions for the niches can be viewed at **www.dailyfutures.com.**

BLUE-CHIP

A higher-class version of a stock is called the blue-chip. This stock is the most reputable publicly traded companies. Many of these companies have an excellent record of accomplishment and have been around for years, making them good for long-term investments. Editors of Wall Street have a reputable Dow Jones Industrial Average, which hosts the top 30 blue-chip companies. Investors can look to their broker; look into a direct stock investment plan, or a dividend investment plan. Profitable and established companies such as Wal-Mart, Coca-Cola, and Exxon Mobile are just a few of the winners, but what people look at is a stock's record, earning power, increases to shares, balance sheets, credit rating, and more.

COMMON

When an investor can invest in a stock that constitutes ownership in a certain corporation, it is a common stock. Participants can invest in newly developed companies or the top dogs, if they wish. Mergers and acquisitions are always taking place. For example, Wachovia recently bought AG Edwards. Shareholders can vote on any issues that may affect the corporation. One vote per share owned is allowed. This includes decisions to the nature of buying a share of another common stock or company, dividend payouts, and stock repurchases. They also are included in board decisions. Believe it or not, the most common stocks are these stocks. In any given situation, if the company goes bankrupt, then creditors, bondholders, and preferred shareholders will be paid first. As a long-term investment, this kind can provide excellent returns, and they outperform most including bonds. While your investment is not guaranteed, the buying and selling of a stock is convenient. The sky is almost the limit for the commons, as there are thousands of them. It is somewhat nice for those individuals who do not have their own company. They can pretend, since there is a proportional share in a company with generating assets; as the business value increases, so does the stock.

Shannon purchased five shares of Google in August, 2004, at $100 per share without considering dividends or splits. As of December, 2007, those shares would be worth $3,496. Likewise, Wal-Mart's stock opened in September, 1970 at $16.50 per share. Since then the company has had 11 two-for-one splits and the stock closed in December, 2007 at $49.

CASE STUDY: KATIE REINSMIDT

CBL & Associates Properties, Inc.

2030 Hamilton Place Boulevard

Chattanooga, TN 37421-6000

Phone 423-855-0001, Fax: (423) 490-8390

Katie_reinsmidt@cblproperties.com
www.cblproperties.com

"Many people speculate that in 2008 there will be a growth in recessions, although we feel the retail market protects us as it provides steady growth opportunities with a solid background offering great returns," said Katie Reinsmidt, director of investor relations. People will dump out of real estate investment trusts (REITS) because the first or second quarter returns do not look promising. Often times what people do not realize is that REITS are meant to be looked at with a long-term perspective, which would also bring better results. The investor community will often get lost in REITS, as the

CASE STUDY: KATIE REINSMIDT

investment horizons do not appear to belong-term when they are. The year 2007 proved to be a fallen-out year in REIT investments, as many investors were reallocating many of their stocks bouncing from one to another. But with a company like CBL & Associates, who represent a mall REIT, this does not affect much due to strong track record and proven performance of its annual growth rate of 12 percent, which has been strong since 2002. A portfolio proves the work you do, and in this case there are 164 retail properties and 84 regional malls, including open-air malls totaling over 83 million square feet. The company went on the public stock market from privatein 1993, and since then dividends to the shareholders have increased, despite many obstacles.

Since going public, CBL has seen an increase in its compound annual growth in which dividends were had increased to at least 8.1 percent or more.

This is not bad. Another thing that supports this is that CBLs management team takes pride by owning over 20 percent of the stocks themselves, meaning there is a lot of confidence in the company. CBL has had success with its common and preferred stocks, and they have recently increased dividends to 7.9 percent as of December, 2007. For the third quarter, which ended September 30, 2007, the company's common stock was at $0.50 per share. The dividends were then paid out by October 15, 2007, to the shareholders. The cash dividend for that quarter was $2.02 per share. In addition, CBL announced a dividend of $0.48 per share for the same period for its preferred stock. This was an approximate $1.80 per share. Likewise, CBLs Series D Preferred Stock saw an annual dividend payout of $1.80 per share. Shareholders on record as of September 14, 2007, received this with both preferred stocks.. Although many people were pulling out of REITS it did not affect CBL. The company refocused its attention to a building year for the retail sector. Results for 2007 were not as strong as 2006. CBL was still busy, however, with $1.5 billion in acquisitions and $340 million in new developments expected to position the future with success. Anomalies in the marketplace can cause any number of factors to make stocks lose a little bit of juice. Such as, a combination of delays with developments caused by hurricanes in 2005 could cause problems where retail stores could not get a permit. Things of this nature can really affect stocks. Because CBL has a proven track record and a strong growth rate, this makes shareholders happy.

CASE STUDY: KATIE REINSMIDT

Each year, CBLs portfolio becomes stronger and is improved with quality. At this point there are approximately seven mall REITS, and a majority of them have an international platform. Just going national this year, CBL has been joint-ventured into China and Brazil. And at this time the company has one of the highest dividend rates in the price sector.

Since 1978, CBLs investment strategy has been to focus on dynamic changing and growing areas where employment bases are logical.

PREFERRED

Preferred stocks also invest in corporations, but shareholders are not involved in change processes. In place, the shareholder gets a fixed dividend (set by the company) somewhere between $25 and $100. The stock is sold at face value. Dividends are affected by the current interest rates set by the FDC. When higher dividends are issued, interest rates are lower, making the stocks more attractive. It does not have as much to offer as common stock, but it is a stable investment vehicle, guaranteeing a timely dividend. While everyone wants a taste of the common, it is not as guaranteed. In addition, an individual investor will have to pay taxes on full dividends received. An advantage a large company has is that it only has to pay 30 percent tax on its full dividends.

Preferred stock can be exchanged for common stock, and the issuer has the right to redeem the investment at all times. The difference between preferred stock and common are the voting rights and a fixed income.

INTERNATIONAL

Some believe it is cheaper to invest in overseas stocks

in what is known as international stock. The risk can be even riskier as currency trades, different economies, governments, and accounting standards do not amount to the U.S. stocks. This can be costly, but that does not mean you should not look into them. Various Web sites are available for those who have a keen focus on the subject matter such as **http://www.global-investing.com**, which teaches the investor good investment moves.

Aside from the U.S. economy, there are at least 20 major stock markets elsewhere. Ten of the largest steel-making companies are not even in the U.S. Something you should know is that in some cases, reporting and tax regulations on securities are different than they would be in the U.S. Foreign countries are not required to provide some details that U.S. companies would provide. An American Depository Receipt (ADR) is meant to make the investment process in the foreign lands a little smoother. It is a certificate issued by a U.S. Bank that represents any number of shares in a foreign stock, and it can be traded on a U.S. Exchange. Capital gains and dividends come in U.S. dollars, while allowing investment in a foreign company at the same time. ADRs are issued by depository banks which hold responsibility on both sides of the transaction. These banks were born in the late 1920s, and the Bank of New York is the largest example to date. Foreign stocks are traded just as U.S. stocks would be. Dividends are paid in U.S. currency.

LUCKY PENNIES?

Like the nickel machines at casinos, penny stocks are available. Most sell at 5 cents or less, and they do not generate large revenue earnings, but on a lucky day you could invest $400 and make $200 or more within just a few days. Information is provided to brokers on pink sheets, an electronic quotation system, which displays quotes from all broker dealers. This practice keeps investors informed of the latest. Penny stocks are considered OTC, as it is security of a small company. They can be traded OTC and through NYSE. Some people believe that is harder to sell penny stocks, as certain quotes cannot be found at a good price. On a good run, you can invest in a stock at a low price with a high growth rate, gaining several hundred percent in a few days although the stocks are considered less liquid. I myself had a lucky moment, gaining a nice short-term investment in just a few days time. But the liquidity issue can cause the stock price to soar or plummet. Since penny stocks can lack in liquidity, prices can vary depending among the spreads.

In the case of the Enron scandal in 2001, the company was a blue-chip stock that plummeted to a penny stock, falling from nearly $100 a share to less than 30 cents within a few months. The company, which was in the top ten of the Fortune 500, represented one of the most successful companies financially as a public company. Many individuals with 401(k) investments were out of luck due to the bankruptcy of Enron. This is a perfect example of how something thought to be so good can go wrong. It was sticky fingers in this instance, however, portraying an example of fraud. A firm once in the top five, Arthur Andersen screwed up big time with the handling and auditing of Enron. This firm gave up its license in 2002 and did not help the economy much either, as over 85,000 people lost their jobs.

Note: the SEC considers a pink sheet stock a risky investment as they are not registered and many statements are not available.

Philicia needed a new guitar and she needed it quick for an upcoming concert. A newsletter she regularly received (with a disclaimer) mentioned a few penny stocks that were worth watching. She took her chances and on a Tuesday bought 1000 shares on at 46 cents a share investing $460 into an Infinity Medical Group penny stock. She then sold the stocks on the following Saturday for $760 netting $300 less the commission which was an approximate $14. In four days, she had enough money to buy a new guitar with a savvy and risky, but quick investment. The following day, her band member tried the same routine in which she purchased 25,000 penny stock shares at nearly 2 cents a piece which quickly dropped below half a cent per share. This stayed this way for a while and eventually the band member sold the stock at a loss because she did not want to lose everything she had originally invested. The initial goal for that investment was to also come out with a new guitar.

CYCLICAL

A cyclical stock mimics the economic trend (business cycles) either picking up speed or decreasing speed profited from businesses. Stocks will rise and fall with business cycles, but the trick is to buy at the low point of the cycle with an expectation of a promising return. These stocks are reliant upon expansion or extraction of the economy.

Seasonal stocks compare to cyclical. This kind goes with retail corporations that do well around the holidays. A non-cyclical stock would be investing in a company that makes an item needed all the time, such as healthcare or a Johnson and Johnson stock. Those guys make everything, and it is important that people have deodorants. A cyclical stock could include an automobile stock. Stocks of this nature are dependent upon the performance of the economy and how much money people have. They mimic business cycles, and fluctuate when there is not necessarily a growth trend, just a pattern. Cyclical stocks are best when the economy looks good, while non-cyclical stocks are those that are needed no matter what.

DEFENSIVE

When the economy is hot, stocks are defensive. This is the same thing as a non-cyclical stock. This type of stock includes those companies that are needed despite what is going on in the world, meaning that if the economy is not doing well these stocks will still provide stable earnings. During a recession period this stock usually provides a nice performance, unless it is in an expansion phase. Electricity, gas, drugs, and food are the staple stocks that usually stay afloat regardless of an uproar in other stocks. However, this type does tend to lag behind in high economic times. If a market downturn is predicted, people tend to invest more in these types, as it is somewhat reliable no matter what.

GROWTH

Growth stocks are encountered when market prices can change quickly. The stocks are meant for growth, but these stocks are also good for long-term opportunities, as dividends are not paid out to investors. Companies spend money on development opportunities instead. This is geared for those with a higher tax bracket because it can help in paying fewer taxes. If you can jump into a successful stock early, the result could be great. These kinds usually have large earning potentials. This also means there could be higher risk, so the cards just have to be played right. When choosing a growth stock, you should look for a positive growth rate, sustainability, and good prices. Look for large companies that have a track record such as Wal-Mart. These funds are involved in corporations expecting a lot of growth with rapid sales and earnings. This can include large or small companies. In recent years, a lot of the success of these funds can be based upon the success of technology – a sector that just keeps getting better and better.

INCOME

A stock that pays more dividends than most is an income stock. This type of stock could bring a month-to-month earning if you play the cards right. Many retirees are fans of this type. Companies involved pay higher dividends than the usual, and a lot of money is distributed through payouts. If interest rates are declining, bonds are the better way to go. Income funds are also called value funds.

A STORY ABOUT COKE...

In 1919 Coca-Cola went public with common stock priced at $40 per share, but a year later it had fallen to $21 per share. However, the stock started rising again. A 100 share purchase at $40 per share in 1919 would be worth several hundred million today. In 1985, the company spent four million dollars on research to find a new formula for a new taste. One reason was that the market share was 24.3

percent in 1980 and by 1984 it had dropped to 21.8 percent. Officials of the company felt that the new formula would boost Coca-Cola's share by 1 percent. However, the market share dropped and 87 days after new Coke was introduced, the old coke was returned to the market. Today, the stock continues to be highly favored. This drink has been around since 1886 selling originally as a soda fountain drink for five cents a glass. Today, a stock share costs $.50. The "Coca-Cola" trademark was registered with the US Patent Office in 1893, and that year was the first year the company paid dividends. In 1928 the sale of coke in bottles exceeded soda fountain sales. Also in the 1920s coke was sold in a six-bottle cardboard carton, which was described as "a home package with a handle of invitation." The hobble-skirt bottle shape was given a registered trademark in 1977. During World War II coke was supplied to the military in foreign countries, and after the war Coca-Cola became a "worldwide symbol of friendship and refreshment." A survey done in 1988 claimed that Coca-Cola has the best-known trademark anywhere in the world. In February 2006, the company had approximately 326,685 accounts on record of people who liked coke-stock.

The company's "Code of Business Conduct" is a guide for employees that exemplify the company's values. It was revised in 2002 to meet the requirements of the Sarbanes-Oxley Act. Coca-Cola is committed to giving consumers the product that best suits a life style and offers more than 2100 products for sale. The company contributes millions to community programs worldwide.

BLENDED FUNDS

This means there is value ad growth funds wrapped in one

opportunity. The average fund is this way. Investing in a fund that serves both categories provides a better edge, making risk less risky.

WHICH WOULD YOU PREFER?

Market capitalization for stocks is the key since it shows the amount of a company's shares outstanding times the stock price. Said simply, it is a company's value. To determine what level stocks are on, brokerages vary according to individual company policies by microcap, small cap, mid cap, and large cap.

Microcap – This stock has less than $50 million.

Microcap stocks trade on both pink sheet and OTC bulletins. Any securities involved are viewable by brokers so long as they are subscribers to the bulletin system. On an OTC bulletin board, investors can research prices, quotes, and volume information. Remember, none of these stocks are regulated under the SEC but are viewed by NASD. Market makers (brokers) use the pink sheet to publish the bid and asking prices of stocks. The SEC has nothing to do with this. Microcap stocks are different from the rest because the companies involved are not big enough to file with the SEC. Public information is not important and no minimum standards must be met. The smaller the stock, the riskier the stock, since the companies involved are typically brand new, never heard of, and have no proven record of accomplishment. Since there is low volume in trading, this really affects the price of the stock. If a company has 500 or more investors and $10 million or more in assets, it must file with the SEC. These companies are typically harder to find. Because the information on these stocks is not readily and publicly available, people are more apt to go for bigger stocks.

Small Cap – This stock is somewhere in the range of $50 million and $1 billion. They tend to rise at a faster pace, expanding revenues and earnings quickly, but this does not mean there are no pitfalls. However, they have strong gains.

Companies that have small caps can be more volatile. The advantage to this type of stock is that they adjust a lot quicker than that of a larger stock. The bad thing is that they are harder to trade and the spreads are bigger. Like microcap stocks, these stocks have scarce information as well. As always, an investor can count on these stocks to provide excellent financial statistics, good business models, and a trusting team. These funds are typical of the investors who are not looking for a long term outcome. Looking back to history, small caps have outperformed the giants, but they are riskier by nature. Sometimes when that smaller company has a successful product, it can outperform the larger company with greater earning potential. When the economy is doing well, so do these stocks, but they do bad when there is any sign of a recession and have a lesser chance of survival than the large cap. The other logical explanation is that consumer confidence is obviously placed with the larger cap companies making the smaller company more risky.

Mid Cap – These stocks are usually in proximity of $500 million to $5 billion. A few companies that fit the profile include Ride Aid Corporation, Black Rock, Allied Capital, Healthcare Property Investors Inc. and several others. In other opinions, it is in the range of $2 and $10 billion. A few companies that fit the profile include Ride Aid Corporation, Black Rock, Allied Capital, Healthcare Property Investors Inc. and several others. While mid cap options are growing, they can be viewed as a safer bet because the companies are less likely to go bankrupt as those of a smaller company and they do n have as much the hassle as the larger cap stocks. This means if the larger cap stocks do not keep up with the competition, they keep up with the mid cap range anyway. The mid caps are really a collection of the smaller stocks. In a bear market, mid caps do well. They tend to outperform other stocks. The mid caps have a better or more solid financial status than that of a large-cap or small-cap making it less of a risk. Mid caps can be viewed as an upgrade for the once small companies who did well.

Large Cap - These stocks contain at least $5 billion total market capitalization, the value of the company. They have smaller growth potential than those smaller caps but they are established and stable. These numbers are not set-in-stone, give or take a few million, but they are pretty close. These stocks are on the highest trading volume lists. They are the most competitive and have the biggest track records. Should the economy bounce around, these stocks are the most affected. People are attracted to these stocks the most because returns are good. The investor just has to be in the right place at the right time. Johnson and Johnson is a large cap example. These companies are blue-chips and overall are less risky than the smaller stocks as they have an established financial background and a reputation. A lot of these giants can be found through the Standard & Poor 500 Index.

THE TRUTH ABOUT BONDS

Bonds are the next best thing to stocks. Bond markets increase when stock markets decrease. They are not as volatile as stocks because they do not go up or down as much as stocks would. They are more stable, and there is less risk involved. Most bonds mature over a certain length of time whereas stocks can go on forever unless a company goes private or bankrupt. The interest payments with bonds are a little bit higher than dividend payments. Bonds are easier to sell off compared to stocks, and twice a year a fixed interest payment is made to the investor. If a bond company were to go bankrupt the shareholder would receive some money back, but not everything. Bonds are loans, which are to be paid back at some point in the future. They are available through foreign or domestic governments, companies, or municipalities. Traders, brokers, and dealers would be happy to help in the secondary market (CMBSs). Brokers are highly favored in bond purchasing. The issuers are the borrowers; they pay you a rate of interest, and at your final maturity you will receive your principal and initial investment. Another advantage is such that investors do not have to pay higher taxes.

If bond rates go up, it is because interest rates have decreased. Logically, when rates go down, interest rates are increasing. An investor will look forward to a new bond with a higher interest rate because it pays out more leaving precedent binds, at a fixed rate, ignored. Long-term bonds are affected more than short-term bonds when this happens. Investors tend to divest from stocks and look to bonds when rates go up as returns seem more attractive sending stock prices down and bond rates up. In all matters, it is vice versa all the time. There are tax-free bond funds that are very similar to regular funds. By investing in mutual bonds, income to the investors will not be taxed. However, there are some state and local taxes that are possible aside from the ones that are completely tax free. Bond funds have expense ratios that vary by fund, but they can be bought through a fund family where there is no commission or load.

Like stocks, there are many choices in bonds too.

S&P RATINGS

INVESTMENT GRADE BONDS	
AAA	Highest Quality
AA	High Quality
A	High-Medium Grade
BBB	Medium-Grade

FIXED RATES

A fixed rate bond insists the market price will decrease in value when the interest rate rises. With fixed payments, this decrease will increase the yield, which is the coupon rate divided by the market price. The coupon rate is the interest rate, while the market price the current value of future interest and principal payments minus the yield, or rate of return. These fixed-term accounts specify a rate of interest for a fixed period. People are attracted to this because they know the money tree will grow. Money is to be left untouched, long-term, and you cannot take any money out. These types of bonds primarily invest in government and corporate debt. Most look to this investment to provide a steady cash flow. These bonds do provide high returns but the risk is still not lacking.

SUBORDINATE

In subordination, this type is inferior to other bonds when there is a case ofliquidation. Senior bond holders are paid before the subordinate holders, making the risk higher. These are usually issued by banks and asset-backed securities. Before the seniors get paid however, the liquidator is paid followed by the government taxes.

PERPETUAL

For those with nine lives, there is also the perpetual kind that has no maturity date. Government officials out of the UK are the most famous. This type goes as far back as 1888, and they are still trading today. There are also ultra long-term bonds which can last several centuries. This class is not redeemable but you get paid by the interest rates. "Some in the U.S. believe it would be more efficient for the government to issue perpetual bonds, which may help it avoid the refinancing costs associated with bond issues that have maturity dates" (**http://pickbrains.com**).

ASSET BACKED

Asset-backed securities equal cash flow from other assets that support the interest and principal payments of this bond. This includes collateralized debt obligations (CDOs), collateralized mortgage obligations (CMOs), and mortgage-backed securities (CMBSs). CDOs gain exposure through a portfolio (mixture of assets) of fixed income assets dividing credit risk, while CMOs have mortgages as collateral issuing bonds as an entity, receiving payments as a common set of rules of an investment bank.

Bonds are often called tranches in these cases. Investors usually include pension funds, mutual funds, government agencies, insurance companies, central banks, hedge funds, and more. Mortgage backed securities, principal, and interest are backed by a mortgage loan. Payments are made on a monthly basis during the lifetime of the loan. Commercial and residential (condominiums and multifamily) are the focus of this kind, and often times state pension funds look to these to further diversify the portfolios. Ginnie Mae is the most common investment option.

Asset-backed securities are usually thought to be a car loan, home equity loan, or lease, which in turn becomes stock. CMBS are thought to be their own niche.

INFLATION LINKED

Inflation-linked bonds portray interest rates that are lower than fixed rate bonds. While principal amounts are growing, the payments increase with inflation. TIPS and I-bonds are U.S. Government examples. The bonds are protected against random inflation. The investor is protected by the Consumer Price Index as it serves as an inflation proxy. The U.S. Treasury has an inflation-protection security (IPS).

The I Bond represents an "inflation-linked" bond. The U.S. Department of Treasury also provides TIPS (Treasury Inflation Protection Securities. While it might be the case that stocks have decreased these bonds are beneficial.

These bonds are not affected as other stocks and bonds are being affected. This type of fund actually prospers during this time since it is a hedge.

TREASURY BONDS & FEDERAL GOVERNMENT BONDS

Where there are U.S. government securities, there are U.S. bonds, treasury notes, or bills. Investors usually feel comfortable investing in these bonds because they feel "safe" essentially investing in the government. That does not mean the securities involved are 100 percent safe from defaulting, although the good thing is that your investments are risk-free. The bad thing is that generally the sought-after returns are in the low-rank category. Yields are usually low, but they increase as the risk does. To learn and enjoy the treasury bonds options, see Treasury Direct at **www.treasurydirect.gov**. These bonds go for about $1,000 to over $25,000. In this instance, these bonds are in the housing industry as either loans or existing mortgages are purchased. These are known as Uncle Sam bonds, or treasury securities; investors must spend at least $10,000 for a treasury bill, while securities may be closer to the $1,000 range, and notes are somewhere in the middle. The most worldwide actively traded interest rate contracts are Treasury futures.

When it comes to savings bonds, there are Series E and Series I bonds, which people who do not have much money to invest can purchase for as low as $25. These bonds mature in 30 years, and at this point the bonds are redeemed automatically and then a zero percent certificate of indebtness is purchased with the proceeds. The government takes care of all of this. If the investor cashes out in the first five years from the time of purchase, then the investor will have a three month penalty. This entails no-interest will be paid for a three-month period. Although these bonds are easy to buy, they may be difficult to value. However, the US government now has an online calculator that can assist. **www.publicdebt.treas.gov/sav/savcalc.htm**. Series E savings bonds are also known as "patriot bonds." They are backed by the U.S. When an investor buys this bond, only half of the face value is paid, meaning $25 would be $12.50. It is just how they are sold. The full face value is received when the bond matures. With Series I, the inflation-indexed bonds, the amount of the bond is adjusted semi-annually. There are two components for this adjustment, and it is designed to show the buying power of investors and the consumer price index. A third option entails a Series HH bond. Interest is paid directly into an account an investor may hold at a financial institution. In ten years time, there is a fixed interest rate, but interest may be earned for up to 20 years.

BOND SOURCES	
These available Web sites offer a multitude of information on all types of bonds, in addition to news and educational material.	
Bondagent.com	www.bondagent.com
BondsOnline.com	www.bondsonline.com
Bondtrac.com	www.bondtrac.com
BMI Quotes	www.bmiquotes.com
Bondpage.com	www.bondpage.com
BondVillage	www.bondvillage.com
Bradynet	www.bradynet.com
Bureau of the Public Debt	www.publicdebt.treas.gov
CNNfn Bond Ceneter	www.cnnfn.com/markets/bodceter
ConvertBond.com	www.convertbond.com

BOND SOURCES	
Fannie Mae	www.fanniemae.com/yields.html
EMuni	www.emuni.com
First Miami Securities	www.firstmiami.com
Garbin Information Systems	www.garbaninfo.com
Ginnie Mae	www.ginniemae.com
GovPX	www.govpx.com
Investing in Bonds.com	www.investinginbonds.com
Kiplinger.com	www.kiplinger.com/ basics/investing/bonds/zeros.html
Lebenthal.com	www.lebenthal.com
Precision Information	www.precision-info.com
Quote.com	www.quote.com
Smith Barney Access	www.salamonsmihbarney.com/ prod_svc/bonds
Stone & Youngberg	www.buybonds.com
The Bond Buyer	www.bondbuyer.com
The Bond Market Association	www.investinginbonds.com
Yahoo!Finance	bonds.yahoo.com/ir_bd4.html

ZERO COUPON

Within a zero coupon bond, there is no interest involved. That is right, no interest. These are fixed-rate bonds minus the coupon. The investor receives the full principal amount in addition to value that has accrued up to the redemption date. A nice lump sum could help pay for your child's college education or assist in retirement. This is meant for a long-term investment. Many of zero coupon bonds do not begin maturing for at least ten to fifteen years. The secondary markets make offers through the U.S. Treasury, corporations, or state and local entities. Do not let the no-interest fool you, because you still have to pay interest upon maturity for any federal, state, or local income taxes.

HIGH YIELD

High-yield bonds are rather risky, as investors expect a higher yield and rate of return rated below the usual investment grade, and there is a risk of default and a risk of downgrade. These are known as "junk" bonds because the yields are higher than those bonds of higher stature. Bonds are rated like a reporter card. A Triple-A means high quality while a D is not so good. It is a credit rating system for credit rating agencies.

S&P RATING

HIGH-YIELD/JUNK BONDS	
BB	Uncertain Outlook (Questionable)
B	Generally Lacking Desirable Qualities
CCC	Poor Quality, Danger of Default
D	In Default

Junk bonds are favored because of the volatility involved and the high-yields. Junk bonds should be purchase when the economy is doing great and consumer spending is high. And logically, anytime there is a recession, junk bonds are not that great of an investment as they become risky. But the upside of these bonds is high returns. However, these bonds should not be used solo, but as a diversification tool for a portfolio. These bonds can score greater returns than the big blue-chip companies and should be held for at least five years because of the volatility. If an employee has a junk bonds through an employer, junk bonds may be less risky because should the company go bankrupt, its remaining assets are distributed making it less risky to the investors. The main thing an investor should keep in mind is that the companies that hold these bonds are more likely to go bankrupt than that of a bigger corporation. Another thing to keep in mind is that a high yield may be good looking but it is due to the investors' of the bond and not the company. It is a reflection of the contributors and the financial situations involved. Another disadvantage of the junk bond is that it lacks in liquidity. Sometimes it is difficult to unload these bonds can be difficult, especially if the market is weak. As a first time investor, investing in junk bonds can be achieved via the advisor who holds your mutual fund. This way the diversification is there and the background information is achieved through someone who understands them better. When choosing a junk bond solo, compare the report card letters and look to see how bouncy the results of the bonds have been.

FLOATING RATE

Floating Rate Notes – Coupons linked to a market index, reset periodically, and made to protect the investors from bouncing interest rates, while carrying lower yields than fixed-note bonds within the same period. Sometimes compared to an adjustable-rate mortgage, however, there is no debt involved here.

BEARER

This is a certificate issued without a name. The person holding the certificate can claim the bond. These can be lost or stolen easily, but the U.S. corporations quit issuing this kind in the 1960s, followed by the U.S. treasury, state, and local tax-exempt bearers in the early 1980s.

MUNICIPAL

Interest is exempt from federal taxes and the income taxes of the state where the bonds were issued in a municipal bond. This type is meant for community efforts, such as schools, parks, and other community projects. However bonds issued for a certain purpose may not be exempt.

This type usually goes for at least $5,000 or more. The states, U.S. Territory, cities, and local government authorities issue this type. Better known as "muni" bonds, interest is paid to the investor for a specific amount of time. Once this is over, the investor will receive the initial investment. With debt securities issued by the government, money is raised by borrowing from investors. Again, timely interest payments are received depending on the denomination and the security. These bonds can be taxed federally, and in some instances may not be taxed locally.

LOTTERY

Lottery Bond – Usually issued out of Europe. Compares much like the fixed-rate bond but the issuer can redeem certain bonds at any given time at higher than face value. Rates of return depend on the lottery-style payouts, which involve a method of randomness. These bonds are compared to lottery tickets because they are drawn monthly to see if you have the "winning" payment. The National Savings Corporation is the only company you should accept these from in the U.S.

CORPORATE

In any case, instead of owning a share of a company, you

are lending money and making money off the interest. This equity fund offers many corporate styles as well as time periods. The U.S. government cannot go bankrupt but companies (ex. Enron) do, so you had better watch out. This type of fund is said to offer a safer risk scale while producing slightly less returns than the government would. These bonds are callable, meaning they can be redeemed at any time. You will be fully taxed with a corporate bond. What is actually purchased is a portion of a large loan. Interest rates are fully specified, and upon repayment a full amount will be paid out on the specified rate. Those payments are made semi-annually.

WEB SITES	
www.bondagent.com	BondAgent.com
www.bondknowledge.com	BondKnowledge.com
www.bondsonline.com	BondsOnline
www.bondresources.com	BondResources.com
www.bondtrac.com	Bondtrac
www.money.cnn.com	CNN/Money
www.bondsonline.com	FAQ Bond
www.garbaninfo.com	Garban Information Systems
www.invetinginbonds.com	InvestingInBonds.com
www.invest-faq.com	The Investment FAQ
www.smithbarney.com	Smith Barney Municipal Bond Inventory
www.bondbuyer.com	The Bond Buyer
www.bondpage.com	Bondpage.com
www.investinginbonds.org	Investor's Guide to Municipal Bonds

WHERE DOES THE MUTUAL FUND FIT IN?

Mutual funds are open-ended investment pools (or portfolios), meaning they hold collections of either stocks, bonds, short-term money market instruments, and other securities, but they mostly invest in stocks and bonds. The funds are willing to accept any new money for the fund at all times. Managers (for an annual fee) trade securities suitable for capital gains or losses while collecting dividends and income, and there is less risk involved than there would be with a stock due to diversification. The result is the earning of an investor. A net asset value is computed daily. This is the net of the fund divided by the number of shares. An initial investment into a mutual fund can range as some may require a minimum of $200, while others suggest at least $10,000. It really caters to the smaller and the larger investors. Sometimes a mutual fund may assist you in starting out small, but it would recommend that the investor keep allocating on a monthly basis to get the best results. The advantage to those funds where individuals invest large amounts is that there are lower expense ratios.

Name	Symbol	1 Year	5 Year	10 Year	Trade Date	Shares	Price Per Share	Gain/ Loss	Value
Example									
Emerging Markets Purchase Fee: 0.5% Redemption Fee: 0.5%	VEIEX	23.00%	32.93%	14.56%	11/22/2005	182	$17.9300	$2,333.14 / $68.43	$5,496.40
Precious Metals & Mining Redemption Fee: 1% if held < than 1 year	VGPMX	33.97%	34.53%	22.53%	11/22/2005	441	$22.6600	$5,252.31 / $52.56	$15,245.37
PRIMECAP Core Fund Redemption Fee: 1% if held < than 1 year	VPCCX	-0.46			11/22/2005	875	$11.4300	$1,146.25 / 11.46%	$11,147.50
EXAMPLE									
Precious Metals & Mining Redemption Fee: 1 % if held < than 1 year	VGPMX	33.97%	34.52%	22.53%	8/14/2006	98	$28.2300	$621.23 / 22.46%	$3,387.86

Since mutual funds are open-ended, at the end of each day the funds issue new shares as some investors may be leaving the fund and others are entering. The share price is then determined by the underlying value of the investments. When an investor leaves, the fund will buy back that person's share. The funds can have over 100 stocks and bonds, in addition to other things. A close-ended fund would have a limited number of shares, trading on the stock exchange as a stock would. An equity fund is the most popular kind of mutual fund. Mutual funds also have micro to large caps based upon what is called the Russell Index — a tracker for global performances on equity investments. Micro cap is approximately $55 million to $550 million and the 2000 index is typically somewhere in the range of $180 million to almost $2 billion. A Midcap index lies between $1.8 billion and nearly $390 billion. Mutual funds can gain some peoples interest for as little as $25 as an investment. Most invest more than that, as the funds are reputable for positive performance. Dividends for mutual funds can be reinvested or taken out in cash.

Leveraging a combination of money secures excellent results. Transaction costs are also cheaper. While the financial advisor of the fund knows what they are doing, the right individual investments within the fund are what make everybody happy.

Mutual funds have not gone bankrupt since 1940, but banks and other savings institutions have. That is 60 years of success. (Cagan, O'Connell, 94). As of 2000, there were over 8,000 mutual fund options. Be aware, though, that hidden costs exist in mutual funds. Do not forget about the taxes. If you lose, logically, you will not be paying on anything, but if you win you pay taxes on dividends and capital gains. State taxes fit in too, depending on which state.

There are 800 real estate companies that focus on many areas, with the Asian Pacific being the most popular. This includes Hong Kong, Japan, and Australia. In reviewing the chart, 25 percent is invested in Europe and the UK, while the biggest portion is invested in the Americas — the biggest of that being the United States and Canada, as well as Latin America and South America.

You must know about the load and no-load mutual funds. One that has a load charges you an initial sales fee upon entrance. This is a front-end loan. The average rate is in the range of 4 percent to 8 percent. That portion of your investment will be the company's commission. In addition, a fee can be charged when you claim your earnings in a mutual fund. This is a back-end loan. Those with no-load, do not charge you for anything. By contrast, a bank or dealer does have the authority to charge a certain fee for the assistance of a sale as a third-party in a mutual fund. Mutual funds have no maturity date and can be redeemed at any time.

The bond, growth, income, balance, index, international, and sector funds are all types of mutual funds. As explained with stocks, the growth funds offer the highest returns with less risk, while the growth and income bond is diversified through a variety of both stocks and bonds. This is also what is meant by a balanced fund. A sector fund is much like future commodities in that you are investing in a specific niche of an industry sector, such as real estate. Index funds indicate a mutual fund that invests in stocks of the highest caliber without too much research.

The previous chart explains the advantage of online investing. It represents 3 different mutual funds and changes made over a period of time. Information is always readily available to online members.

After meeting the minimal requirement for investing in a mutual fund, look at that funds prospectus to see if they have an automatic investment plan (AIP). The benefits of this are a preset amount of money is deducted from an investors checking or savings account and are then invested in a mutual fund of you choice. This may also be called dollar cost averaging. The profit is usually better this way because more shares can be purchased when or if share prices are down and fewer shares when prices are up. This withdrawals can range anywhere from $50 to only $100,000 per month, if the investor would like.

EXAMPLE

Tyffani invested an approximate $27,000 with Vanguard in December 2002. She then dispersed this amount among three funds which had a positive performance for the next five years. The first year, the rate of return for all accounts was 24.9 percent, the third year had a return of 17.7 percent and year five saw a return of 14 percent. Nearly five years later, her original investment had increased nearly $20,000 to $45,200. As of November 2006, those accounts were at an approximate $36,200 and for that period she had a dividend payout of around $2,300, which she then reinvested. From that time period the mutual funds had increased in value by $6,700. Adding this to the dividend is an approximate $9,000 which brings the total value to $45,000. All three are foreign mutual funds. One, for example, invests its money in mining stocks. Foreign stocks are volatile in that, if a war breaks out in Latin America, for example, the mutual fund *could go belly-up overnight. Another example of making a lot of money that can be lost quickly, too.*

EXPENSE RATIOS

Expense ratios for mutual funds are determined by the percentage of the assets. The expenses are contributed to keeping the fund running, in addition to administrative costs, an advisory fee, and distribution fees. For example, 12-b1 distribution fees are for marketing and advertising costs. Not all mutual funds have the same expenses, but those with a 12b-1 mean the investor automatically becomes an advertiser with no hands-on experience. The average mutual fund expense rate is at least 1.5 percent, but it could be more. This is where the mutual fund itself makes its money. With administrative costs, this includes office activities such as customer service, mailings, record keeping, and anything else relevant in the office.

Depending on the firm, these costs can vary, and since you need a manager or an advisor to run the fund, fees in this area can range, too. All of these things are combined, making it easier for the investor that does not want to do the math. Most investors do not break these ratios down into detail because they are unavoidable, and the specifics are not particularly important. However, the costs of funds may very tremendously; if you compare some of the top brands such as Merrill Lynch or Vanguard, you can get an idea of the variety of costs. If the companies you are considering have equivalent records, it would seem logical to go with the one with fewer expenses, although there may be a good reason why one firm costs more. If the investor is looking into a company where there are small-cap growth specialties, expenses will be higher due to more research and active trading, while index funds tend to be cheaper. An equity fund usually has a higher expense ratio than a fixed-income fund. International stock funds usually have higher expense ratios than domestic funds, and funds that are actively managed will have a higher expense ratio than index funds.

Growth and income-type mutual funds have an average expense ratio of 1.29 percent. If there is a 10-year investment of $10,000 in this fund the expenses will be $1,183. A mutual fund which copies the S&P 500 index, and has an expense ratio of 0.12 percent, would charge $154 in ten years for an investment of $10,000. If the investor had either one of these two funds for 40 to 50 years, the obvious choice in the expense ratio would be the second fund because it is cheaper. Some mutual funds charge different amounts by classes in investment choices. The prospectus for the mutual fund will give you the funds fees and expenses. Again, it tells you the objectives and expectations for risk as well as performance. There are three classes of shares among some funds which shares are categorized by A, B, and C.

EXAMPLE

Judy wanted to invest some money into a mutual fund for her daughter Morgan. She was having difficulty deciding which type of shares to go with. Looking at the Class A shares, they had a front-end sales charge. That means if you invest $10,000, part of that will automatically go to a sales charge. Meanwhile a class B share did not charge a front-end sales charge in this case, although B did charge a deferred charge when an investor was ready to sell shares. These sales charges appeared to be higher than class A.

Class C shares offered no sales charges at the beginning of a purchase, but the catch here was that sometimes there is a small charge should the investor decide to sell the stocks involved within a short period of time. To Judy, it seemed that class C was the right way to go since she was not planning to sell right away. Confusion still struck Judy because she was told if she held the shares in class C for too long the general management expenses could actually add up to be more than the rest. Looking into class B and A again, A still seemed to be the best, even though there was a front-end sales charge because B usually has higher asset-based charges and a sales charge at the end. In class A, the mutual fund may offer discounts. If Judy makes a large purchase or has other mutual funds with that company or agrees to regularly purchasing more funds for the rest of her kids, then she may be offered a discount on a front-end sales charge. These discounts are often called **breakpoints.**

EXAMPLE	
CLASS A	front-end sales charge
CLASS B	no front-end sales charge, but a deferred charge
CLASS C	no front-end sales charge, but a small charge in selling stocks

EQUITY, FIXED-INCOME OR MONEY MARKET MUTUAL FUNDS

The Government National Mortgage Association (Ginnie Mae) created in the 1960s, and the Federal Home Loan Mortgage Association (Freddie Mac) along with the Federal National Mortgage Association (Fannie Mae), are all involved in the sale of mortgage-backed securities. It is usually the larger investors who are involved in this type of investment, but these mortgages have been collaborated into all types of securities, including mutual funds. Fixed-income mutual funds invest into mortgage-backed securities. Making a long story short, there are three types of mutual funds. A fixed-income mutual fund investment invests in bonds, an equity fund investment for stocks, and then there are money market funds.

A *money market fund* is a debt investment in which maturity is less than one year and the result is a lot of liquidity. Treasury bills make up the majority of these instruments, and they are known for being risk free. Treasury bills are issued by the U.S. government and are short-term obligations. No interest is paid, and they are sold at a discount of the face value, which brings good returns. They are sold on a week auction conducted by the Federal Reserve System. An interest rate is discounted from the price of the bill and you will receive nothing until the bill expires. At this point, you receive both principal and interest. There are also treasury bonds, notes, and Treasury Inflation Protected Securities (TIPS) issued by the government. They can also be bought at an auction. Notes have a maturity period of two to ten years. Coupon payments are made every six months. Also known as T-Notes, these securities have denominations anywhere from $1,000 to $1,000,000. The TIPS is also a note that offers protection from inflation, as there is a higher rate of return with comparison to the inflation to the maturity date. It also pays interest semiannually, and the principal is paid upon maturity. TIPS have a reputation of being the safest with lower returns. TIPS have constant coupon obligations, and they are offered via five, ten, and twenty-year maturity dates.

DIVIDEND REINVESTMENTS AND SPLITS

A dividend reinvestment plan, or DRIP, increases your investment because as you receive your dividends, you can reinvest that into more shares. Most of the time these shares are commission free or at a discounted price compared to the actual price. You are purchasing shares or even fractions of shares, and you can spend as little as $10 while doing this. You can use any amount of money. A company will notify customers a certain time of year when this action is allowed. All shares involved are purchased by the broker in the secondary market, and those shares come out of the bucket of shares that belong to that firm. Another advantage to DRIPs is that they are commission free, and when you purchase shares from a company there is a small discount, even if they are facilitating the shares. Discounts are anywhere from 1 percent to 10 percent. If you focus your shares to an IRA retirement account, you can shelter dividends from current tax liability. Some people think that because you do not actually see dividends since they are reinvested, you are not taxed on them. There are taxes, though; it is considered income no matter what. A lot of times, dividend reinvestment plans are part of a stock purchase plan.

With splits, a company's outstanding shares are increased without changing a shareholders' equity. The advantage is that the shareholders investments increase, but the total values do not. When dividends are paid out by the company, they are reduced the fit the portion of that particular split. The options make the investment seem more affordable to investors while the liquidity is increased. A buyer would most likely go with 20 shares as $1 than one share at $100, but the type of investor would play a factor too. Lower stock prices may seem more appealing to some investors, and in some cases buying in smaller shares may mean lower brokerage commissions. Stocks can be split 2-for-1, 4-for-3, five-for-2, or 3-for-2. In making comparisons with DRIP portfolios, try **www.dripadvisor.com.** Here, you will be able to view different stocks at various monthly savings. In opposite, a company can exchange a share of stock for a larger number of outstanding shares. A company does this in an attempt to reduce the number of outstanding shares. This is a reverse split.

WEB SITES

DRIP Investor
www.dripinvestor.com

Moneypaper
www.moneypaper.com

National Association of Investors Corp
www.naicstockservice.com

Net Stock Direct
www.netstockdirect.com

HEDGE FUNDS

There will come a time when an investor will hear about hedge funds.

Hedging alone is terminology that every investor should be aware of. Funds that are hedge can gin a stronger performance for a fund than those that are not hedged. Hedge funds are "private investment funds" in which good returns are achieved through both good and bad markets. As an alternative investment, these funds are managed through professional managers, specific to this type. They do gain a percentage of the profits the investor gains as does most brokers, but with great performance, an investor can become comfortable. A unique trait of hedge fund manager to assure investors' is that they invest their own money into hedge funds making the investor more confident about investing into a hedge fund. Hedge funds like may other investment options are meant to gain attractive returns, but are meant for a long-term capital growth. The goal of a hedge fund is to exceed inflation. This can be done in both an aggressive and conservative manner.

In comparing the hedge fund to the mutual fund, the difference is the assets that are involved. In most cases, hedge fund assets are smaller than those involved in a mutual fund. Mutual funds can not participate in short-term trading but hedge funds can. Hedge funds are super risky. They go against the odds. The U.S. equity market is a major player in addition to the international equity market, an increasingly popular investment. The top dogs in hedge funds are the larger investors including pension funds, large corporations, funds of funds managers, endowments and foundations, insurance companies, banks and broker-dealers. Since we are more involved on the broker dealer portion, let's focus on that. With a brokerage firm, online or not, as individuals your advisor can assist as it is another investment alternative for diversification. It is the high-net-worth individuals that invest in hedge funds however because it takes a lot of money to invest in a hedge fund to begin with. Grant it hedge funds have the same investment objectives as a mutual fund as nice returns are the primary goal and the asset classes involved are very similar. When referring to assets, this includes equities, fixed-incomes, cash and equivalents, and alternatives. Equity assets include common and preferred stocks while fixed income is when a loan is made to a corporation and is then viewed as debt. All in all, hedge funds are not for the average investor, but for those with more money and that can associate with a much more extreme high risk. There is a limited range of qualified investors.

DIRECT PUBIC OFFERINGS

A DPO is the opposite of an IPO. A company can market shares in direct connection with its own shareholders, which can include distributors, friends, suppliers, and employees. They are a different route from IPOs, as a company can sell shares to the favored beforehand, as well as prospective clients. DPOs are a less expensive route to take compared to how offerings are usually made following underwriting standards. DPOs are not in conjunction with banks or venture capital financing for those qualified businesses. The good thing about DPOs is that the company has complete control over the target community it wishes to reach. It gives a company complete advantage over business strategies in a positive way, while increasing customer satisfaction. DPOs are still registered under the SEC, but they are different from a traditional stock. Stock is sold in a company to individual investors through either a public or private placement of shares with an exception of underwriting fees. Thousands of dollars are saved by not having underwriters. Raising capital with this type of offering is much less expensive. Other advantages to DPOs are a lack of having to pay broker commissions, and the entire process of investing this way is typically faster. Businesses involved in this movement include consumer market products. This can include beer, food, and many other things. The only difference between an IPO and a DPO is the amount of financing involved. Under SEC regulations, a DPO has to have at least $5 million raised over a year's time, minus the costs, which reduces that to $3 million. Critics feel that DPOs are a bad way to go, regardless of the SECs approval, since the backbone of professionalism is not that strong. This means there is not too much involvement by stockbrokers, lawyers, bankers, and others who support the role of an IPO and ensure more security. Critics also feel that DPOs are not priced at market value as an IPO would be. Once upon a time, the investor could only purchase these stocks if he/she lived in the same state in which a specific company was located. As long as that company is registered in your state then there will be no problems. With the ever-so-popular Internet these offerings are made available everywhere. The trait of a DPO is such that when the stock is volatile, the value can triple the amount it started in no time, making it a nice investment. DPOs are really not for the first-time investor because a lot of money can be lost quickly. DPOs offer subscription agreements in the company's prospectus, and this is how you can order your shares. Once that is done, in about a week's time the investor receives a confirmation via mail, which is the followed by a stock certificate.

DIRECT PURCHASE PLANS

There is also a Direct Purchase Plan (DPP). This does not have anything to do with a DPO. DPPs are publicly-traded companies with a history of accomplishment. Often they are called no-lean stock plans, as an investor can get into a direct purchase plan. This allows for reinvestment opportunities with the dividends. DPPs are meant for long-term investors. Another difference from a DPO is that there are initial investment fees, including per-transaction fees, enrollment fees, account management fees, and selling fees. Never forget to read the fine print. In comparison to a DRIP, you can be a first-time buyer with a DPP, whereas with a DRIP you need to have already reinvested dividends for more stock shares. The idea of the DPP did trickle from the DRIP system, however. The biggest advantage to investors would be the direct investments to a company rather than to a broker. DPPs are another example of a no-load stock, although you may have to pay a fee to set up a stock purchase account even though you are avoiding the broker fees. These stocks are also SEC regulated. A stock purchase account is also known as a direct stock purchase plan, or DSP. This is the program in which the SEC regulates the investments made to these companies minus the broker fees. Investors are also attracted to DPPs since the initial investing opportunity is cheaper, and smaller amounts of money can be allocated. It is considered a public offering. An excellent Web site to start researching both DPPs and DRIPS is **http://www.wall-street.com/directlist.html.**

EXCHANGE TRADED FUNDS

Becoming popular in the late 1990s, exchange traded funds (ETF) are an alternative route for investors, as they trade similarly to stocks on all major exchanges, except they are index funds. In an ETF open-ended companies can trade at all hours of the day, constantly, aside from the Wall Street hours. Groups of shares (baskets) are put together by choice of the investors in which their choices compare to that of a particular index of any type, for all asset classes. It offers instant exposure to many portfolios. There is no fund manager in this situation, just the investors. In most cases, these funds consist of several, rather than few, stocks or fixed-income securities, which are index-linked and not actively managed. This can have a range of several thousand stock shares depending on any given instance, and the bundle is traded as an individual stock that represents the thousands of shares. That said, the Standard & Poor's Depository Receipt is a great example on the AMEX with the ticker symbol SPY; there are at least 150 options.

These so-called "Spiders" are run by an individual company on an index, although the ETF is based on the S&P 500 index. But let us not forget the Dow Jones Industrial Average in addition to the NASDAQ composite, both of which are also good starts. The goal is duplication of other portfolios to try to gain the same returns for the investors. As diversification is always the goal, ETFs offer this in a mutual fund way but have features that a stock would. There are also ETFs that look at daily performances with elevated benchmarks which bring more integrated advantages. There are an approximate 40 funds among a few of the main indexes. It may be the case that negative benchmarks are what it takes to meet the desired goal. What makes ETFs attractive to investors is that there is something out there for everyone. The choice is readily available for REITS, large and small companies, bonds, stocks, and other commodities in indexes for small to large cap, as well as fixed income options.

Going in, expense ratios are lower for investors, as it easy to manage as a long-termed investment, and annual fees are cheaper than that of a typical mutual fund. Selling-short and hedging strategies are part of the game, too, for those who wish to make a quick profit. Short ETFs are beneficial in that investors can profit from declines in underlying indexes without direct security, short-selling as the value of a certain index could go down. ETFs are protected by the SEC just as stocks, but some things differ since transactions are not similar to stocks. While there are costs going in no matter what, online discount brokers are called "discount" for one reason or another with negotiable prices depending on the trades. Another advantage to ETFs is that they are available to everyone worldwide on an open market, while the standard open-ended mutual fund in the U.S. is available to only those that live in the U.S. With an ETF, however, an investor outside the U.S. can participate in the U.S. mutual funds. Other countries that are big on this option include Australia, Canada, Europe, Finnish, Hong Kong, Japan, Korea, Singapore, Sweden, and Turkey.

As an example, an energy commodity will have different percentages invested in oil companies, weighted by market capitalization. Dividends are paid out to the investors just as a stock dividends are. ETFs are also more tax efficient than mutual funds. In most cases, investors are only affected by the capital gain taxes as if they are selling their own shares. Since the amount of capital gains are declared, this saves taxes. Since ETFs are transferred securities among the individual investor, there are no tax consequences to the fund. Also, there is no minimum investment with an ETF, and you can buy on margin. What this means is that the same terms are applied to that of a stock, where an amount of money can be borrowed based on the market value of an account. The Federal Reserve Board sets these percentages, and, given any price drop in your security, a brokerage firm can make a "margin call" whereby an investor deposits more funds, and more liquidation is made for the securities.

A FEW TOP US ETFS: 4Q 2007	
DIAMONDS Trust, Series 1 (AMEX:DIA)	Diamonds
Energy Select Sector SPDR (AMEX:XLE)	Spiders
Financial Select Sector SPDR (AMEX: XLF)	
SPDRs by State Street Global Advisors (AMEX: SPY)	
iShares Dow Jones US Real Estate (NYSE: IYR)	
iShares S&P 500 Index Fund (NYSE: IYR)	
PowerShares QQQ (Nasdaq: QQQQ)	Cubes

There are more pros than cons with ETFs. It is important to be aware that some country funds and sector-focused funds may have larger bid-ask spreads. But those that are low bid-ask would compare to something of the blue-chip stock. A bid-ask spread is the difference among the highest price a buyer is willing to pay and the lowest price a seller is willing to sell a stock. Whatever the difference is the spread. The expense ratio and its mirrored-index are some of the first observations to make when going into an ETF.

REGARDING INTERNATIONAL INVESTMENTS, ONLINE

An American Depository Receipt is a way for Americans to purchase and trade foreign securities. These ADRs were first introduced in Britain in 1927. Generally, to maintain and list ADRs on a United States exchange, an investment bank and a depository bank are involved. The investment bank arranges to buy shares on a foreign market and then issues them in the U.S. The depository bank, handles the ADR certificate issuance and cancellation process that are backed by investors' orders of shares, but this bank does not sale the ADRs. ADRs are negotiable U.S. money designating instruments and are usually listed with the letter A. This type of investment can be traded online. NASDAQ and the NYSE are at least two sources where ADRs are available. They can be purchased through an online broker by paying a commission. Another option is to go through an investment bank such as JP Morgan, a leader in this type of investment. Often times ADRs may be purchased online without a broker. Dividends from the payouts are always paid in U.S. currency. If the U.S. dollar becomes stronger, it will cause a decrease in value of the foreign investment. The reverse would be true if the U.S. dollar declines leaving the foreign investment to increase. Additionally, ADRs are not risk-free investments because of currency changes or unstable environments. An example of this could be a revolution or civil war. It is also possible that a government can take control of a company in the foreign countries simply because they can. Another way to invest in foreign markets is with mutual funds. Foreign mutual funds can be load, no-load, open-end, or closed-end. Open-end funds can be any combination of convertibles, bonds, or equities. Meanwhile, close-end funds can be any combination leaning toward capital gains or income. Regional funds, single-country funds, emerging market funds, global funds, and international funds represent the different categories with international mutual fund investments. Regional funds focus on specific areas while single-country funds represent exactly as the title says. Emerging markets however are those that are shifting from agricultural to industrial matters or possibly from a government to a free enterprise where all can own a company. Global funds which are a fairly hot topic lately combine the foreign and U.S. investments. An "international" option in a mutual fund investment choice means there are no U.S. equities included.

WEB SITES

www.adr.com

wwss.citissb.com/adr/www

www.eftconnect.com/select/cef/global.asp

www.emergingportfolio.com

www.irasia.com

www.adrbny.com

www.morningstar.com

www.site-by-site.com

www.funds-sp.com/win/en/Index.jps

YOUR INDIVIDUAL RETIREMENT ACCOUNTS (IRAS)

IRAs are the most popular type of retirement account. There are two types of IRAs: traditional and Roth. The traditional ones will allow you to save $5000 per year beginning in 2008. If you are married, each spouse will be allowed to save $4000 per year in separate accounts. Traditional IRAs allow for a tax-deductible contribution in addition to a tax-free earning. They are held by a bank or an institution in which a custodian makes a certificate of investment or CD, or a brokerage may invest in stocks and mutual funds. Your IRA is protected by the U.S. Supreme Court if you go bankrupt. You pay taxes when you begin deductions. Your standard IRA can be converted to a Roth. To do this, you must have an adjusted gross income of $100,000 or less. You must also include any assets that are taxable into that number, and by doing this you can avoid any taxes on future earnings or withdrawals, however you will pay taxes on any conversions or distributions. To make a long story short, you are earning tax-free benefits from the growth you gain in the Roth account.

In a Roth IRA you prepay taxes, so you do not pay when it is time to take the money out. Your income must be between $95,000 and $110,000 single tax returns, or around $160,000 on a joint tax return. You will pay a penalty if you take extra money earned out of your IRA before you are 59½ unless you use it for a first time home purchase, or become disabled.

Once you reach this point, you can withdraw as you please from your savings, but when you reach 70 1/2, if you have not taken anything out of your IRA then you must start to withdraw or pay a penalty. Individuals can contribute to a traditional IRA regardless if they have other retirement plans. Anyone can have an IRA in addition to other retirement plans. The catch is that employee contributions cannot always be deducted if his or her spouse had his or her own plan as well.

For those who are self-employed, SEP IRAs are available. The difference is that the pension fund account is not in a company's name but in the employee's name. There are certain provisions such as age, income, and work period. More information can be found through the Internal Revenue Service at **http://www.irs.gov/pub/irs-pdf/ p560.pdf**. In addition, there is what is called a Simple IRA, Savings Incentive Match Plan for Employees, in which an employer-provided pension plan can allow both employee and employer contributions, as does the 401(k). These IRAs cannot be transferred to another retirement plan but you can convert it to a Roth. A Self-Directed IRA, requires the actual plan to be in charge of making investment decisions — a holder of your property on behalf of a beneficiary (or company), in which investment decisions are made. This is much like an advisor to the real-estate portfolio for a pension fund; you just let them do all the work. Not only are stocks involved, but also real estate, mortgages, franchises, partnerships, and private equity. More information can be found through the Internal Revenue Service Web site.

Some of us just do not want to be bothered with things. Those who do not wish to manage their own IRA, there are professionally managed options offered by online brokerages.

WEB SITES FOR 401(K) INFORMATION

DirectAdvice
www.directadvice.com

Financial Engines
www.financialengines.com

www.MonteCarloSimulations.org
Morningstar's ClearFuture

www.morningstar.com
mPower

www.mpower.com
Quicken 401K advisor

www.quicken.com

EXAMPLE

Betty graduated from college at the age of 22 and went to work for a large company. After being with this company for eight years she has received several promotions and salary increases. Becoming aware that in the current year she will be making $85,000 she also knows that she has no significant tax write-offs. She has enjoyed spending her money on a nice two bedroom apartment, a nice car, lots of clothes, going out in the evenings with friends. She has also spent money on her two cats who are very pampered when she is home. She has come to the realization that she is in her 30s (just barely) and needs to do something to save more money, find a good tax write-off and ensure her future retirement needs. She decides to spend less time going out at night and more time on her high-tech computer looking for ways to save taxes and making the best investments. She found that there were a lot of Internet sites offering suggestions for saving money and explaining the 401(k), IRAs and Roth IRAs. She has decided to make three significant changes. She had been maxing out her 401(k) as her only investment. Her company matches 6 percent of her salary, which will be $5100 in the current year. Since a 401(k) is pre-tax she will *only contribute as much as the company matches although this means a smaller tax write-off now. Tax rates are fairly low now but with changes in government administration they may go up in the future. Other money she wants to save can go to a Roth IRA which is after-tax. That means that when she is able to withdraw the money the taxes have already been paid. The third investment change is to save as much money as possible toward a down payment on a house as this will be the largest tax saving she can make. She and her cats live happily ever after.*

ESTATE PLANNING

Dan was a single guy living at home with his father and working in the family business.

When he found out he was going to inherit a fortune when his sickly father died, he decided he needed a wife with which to share his fortune.

One evening at an investment meeting, he spotted the most beautiful woman he had ever seen. Her natural beauty took his breath away.

"I may look like just an ordinary man," he said to her, "but in just a few years, my father will die, and I'll inherit 20 million dollars."

Impressed, the woman obtained his business card and three days later, she became his stepmother.

Women are so much better at estate planning than men. ~Author Unknown

OTHER INVESTMENT OPTIONS

A 529 plan is "a qualified tuition plan." Anyone can open them for themselves or for anyone else. There is a tremendous tax advantage savings, and earnings with this plan are not subject to federal taxes, and in many cases state taxes as well, as long as it is used as intended.

Withdrawing the money for any other reason may cause taxes and a penalty. One type is prepaid tuition, where you can purchase credits at participating colleges and universities; the other type is the college savings plan that permits an "account holder" to establish an account for "the beneficiary," whomever you buy it for. The sole purpose of this plan is to pay for the expenses of going to college. The account holder has some say in choosing the investments (stocks), but individual states decide what is in the portfolios. It could be either a bond fund or a mutual fund. Under the Uniform Gifts to Minors Act and the Uniform Transfers to Minors Act, the custodian of any kind of fund for minors is usually the parents or grandparents. The advantages of these Acts are such that portions of the earnings are free from federal tax and portions are taxed at the child's tax rate, meaning they are taxed at the very minimum as opposed to the rate the parents or grandparents may be taxed. The custodian must be responsible for managing the money invested in these funds as well as they can. The disadvantage to the custodian is that they have to turn over the assets to the child, and they cannot reclaim the money for themselves.

In a 529 plan, parents resume full control of the fund even after that child has begun going to college. This is to ensure that the money is actually used for college tuition or what have you. These plans are different in that any amount of money can be contributed and parents are not taxed for it. Aside from the fact that people get tax breaks on these funds, the parents can further expand the benefits to the state income taxes where they can also claim their contributions which gives a deduction.

There are some disadvantages however with the 529 plan. Some plans prohibit investors from transferring from one fund to another. Investors' can switch plans to other states once a year under certain conditions. Many states offer 529 plans and you do not have to purchase one in your own state. These plans can be easily purchased through brokers should an investor not want to do the research on his own. Asset allocations can vary among each state and some may seem more conservative than others. Regarding taxes, rumor has it that the tax benefit could disappear in 2010.While most portfolios have all sorts of diversification, it might be a different story with a 529 plan because it is not an option. Plans tend to have specific choices and once you are in, there is no switching around with the plan like possible rollovers with 401Ks. In choosing a 529 plan, things consider are investment options, manager of the plan, yearly expenses, minimum and maximum contributions, tax deduction options, withdrawal procedures, and account rules.

There are also Educational IRAs. Here you can also save for college, tax-free. Up to $2,000 a year may be allocated to this plan for children under the age of 18. With a 529 plan however, there is no limit. Another difference from the 529 plan is that the educational IRA is more flexible and a contributor can invest in all asset classes on the condition that the IRA is gained through a brokerage firm, a mutual fund company, or any other financial institution. Transferring to other funds is not as big of an issue with a 529 plan and if one child does not use all the money for college in one instance then the other children can use it for their college funds. Additionally, these funds are not just geared for college. They can be used for other school expenses such as elementary tuition. This may also include extra expenses for tutoring and sports. And there are always pros and cons with everything. In this instance, a parent with triplets would have to have three different educational IRAs and not just one for all of them. The biggest disadvantage is a student could be denied financial assistance during the college years due to the fact there is an educational IRA. The student may be able to receive some financial help, but not much. Likewise, if your son is 30, and he is still going to college, the IRS could treat the account as a distribution, subject to income taxes and or penalties. It is almost like the IRS is saying the student should have been graduated already. Enough is enough, I guess.

AND YOUR 401(K)S

This is an employer-sponsored retirement plan that is under the direction of the Internal Revenue Service. Employees can choose specificities in which a certain portion of your paycheck goes to this plan until withdrawal time. Most are participant directed where you can choose from stocks, mutual funds, and more for diversification, and in most cases these decisions can be changed. These plans are tax-deferred until you begin withdrawing, and they are protected by the Employee Retirement Income Security Act (ERISA), which means the plan is protected by creditors and other entities. Employers may make matched contributions at a certain percentage of the amount you contributed, depending on company policy.

ERISA was established in 1974 to create guidelines on the tax rules for retirement plans. It protects both the individual and beneficiaries (family), as all financial information for the plan is disclosed in addition to any needed remedies having to do with the court. The Internal Revenue Service, Department of Labor, and Pension Benefit Guaranty Corporation all take a part with ERISA. The Act began to take effect in 1974 when President John F. Kennedy created a pension plan committee. Due to poorly funded and run pension systems, by September 2 that same year President Gerald Ford enacted ERISA. It was Labor Day.

The difference between a 401(k) plan and a mutual fund is that the IRS does not tax a 401(k) until you begin withdrawing. You are eligible to sign up for 401(k) within some companies after a certain period. As of 2005, you can invest up to $14,000 of your salary to a plan per year (Cagan, 196). If you should decide to change career paths, your 401(k) can stay with you as tax-deferred, and it can also be transferred among new employment. If this does not apply, you may roll it into an IRA. There are time periods and penalties if you chose to do these things, depending on the situation. The 401(k) is similar to the IRA in that at 59 ½ years of age you are eligible to begin using your retirement and then at 70 1/2 means the government will service you.

EXAMPLE

Jade started a new job at the age of 27 making $50,000. She knew she needed to start saving for her retirement so she started investing in a 401(k) where she allocated 11 percent per year out of her paycheck which equals $5,500. In order to have that same amount of income by the time she retires 40 years later, 11 percent would be appropriate to reach that goal. If she were to wait until she was 37 years old before beginning to save, then the percentage would need to be at least 16 percent in order to reach that goal, and likewise when she turned 47 years old it would need to be 28 percent since there would be a lot of catching up to do. The verdict is, the younger you start, the better the investment. It is difficult to determine exactly how much she will actually have at retirement since she had several raises, each of which caused the investment to go up as more money was contributed. In addition, 401(k) investments vary leaving it difficult to pinpoint exactly how much she will have in the long-term. If you took this money and put it under you mattress instead of a 401(k) you would have at least $220,000 cash going by $5,500 (annually) multiplied by 40 years. That is almost five years of a $50,000 income, but she wants to travel too so it is important to invest to make even more money.

https://personal.vanguard.com/VGApp/hnw/planningeducation/retirement/PEdRetInvHowMuch-ToSaveContent.jsp#early

EX. 2

In 1970, 401(k)s and IRAs did not yet exist, but there were retirement plans. Patricia and William were friends working for the same company, both were making $15,000 a year. The employee could contribute up to 12 percent of their salary per year, and if they contributed that amount the company would match 2 percent of that. There was a savings plan by the company that paid 8 percent per year. Initially, William invested $2,100 and at the end of four years, he had saved $10,220. Patricia, on the other hand, decided she would rather spend more money on clothes and only saved 5 percent of her salary for the plan. Because she did not invest the full 12 percent, the company did not match anything. While her original investment was $750, at the end of four years she had only saved $3,650.

EX. 3

Bubba, 38- years- old and single, has been working for a non-profit company the past 6 years and has a 403(b) plan. He has been seriously dating and thinks this woman may be someone he wants to marry and have children with. Although he enjoys his job with the non-profit company his salary is not as high as he would like and there is very little room for advancement. After interviewing with two for-profit companies he has been offered a job that seems suitable for his current and future salary needs. Now he needs to decide what to do with his 403(b) plan. He does not want to cash out and pay taxes so what should he do - put it in the 401(k) with the new company or go with an IRA Rollover. After asking two friends their opinions (one said IRA Rollover, the other said 401(k), he decided to spend a little money and get the opinion of a financial planner. The advice given to him was a definite roll over into an IRA at a brokerage or discount brokerage firm for the following reasons. A 401(k) usually consists of mutual funds and/or employer's stock. Because of Bubba's age and thoughts of future family he was advised to become more conservative about the type of his investments which would include the purchase of bonds. The financial planner was very much against bond mutual funds as they have a high expense ratio and no maturity date. Individual bonds cannot be purchased in a 401(k). With an IRA Rollover Bubba can buy individual bonds that have no expense ratio, but have a maturity date and a lock-

in interest rate. He can also make other types of investments for his IRA Rollover.

403B

The downside of a 403B is that there is no investing in stocks. Money is set aside via salary reduction agreements with employers on a pretax basis. A financial institution handles the plan similar to a 401(k) as it is tax-deferred until retirement. It would be taxed as ordinary income. Since the 401(k) and 403B compare in a lot of ways, people get confused. Regarding a pre-tax basis, both plans are the same as is the tax law pertaining to them. The 401(k)s are geared for those workers that are in a private sector. There is an exception to the rule with some employees, but those that make the cut include religious groups, charity groups, and educational groups, for example. Public schools, hospitals, and libraries may also be in the mix. A 403b7 is made of mutual funds while other options include variable annuity contracts with an insurance company, or a retirement account for a church.

INDEX FUNDS

Index funds track themselves. It sounds a little strange but they were started because institutional investors wanted to see how their managers were doing. Do not buy an index fund until you know what the indexes contain. Index funds will not be at the top of the money-makers but neither will they be at the bottom. Over several years they may outperform actively managed funds and steadily make money. Of course, since they track other funds, they will drop in value the same as regular mutual funds with a down market but will rise in value with an up market. Index funds are a good investment for people who do not have enough ready cash to invest in a variety of regular mutual funds. You can get all the different type of stocks rolled up in one index fund by choosing that type of fund. If you are interested in a specific industry such as real estate, utilities, technology, etc. there are index funds that are tied to those businesses. The expense ratio for index funds is lower than stock funds and the tax benefits are better. With mutual funds you may have to pay short term capital gains because of the constant trading. Quite a few of the index funds tend to do very little trading so they might not have any short term tax costs. Be sure to read the prospectus on a fund you are interested in to find the fee schedule. Some of the newer funds have a sales commission (load). Small cap and foreign index funds may not be as good an investment as the large cap. Index funds that contain a large number of smaller companies tend to be more volatile, also funds that specialize in one industry. Possibly the most volatile are called leveraged index funds. These are meant to perform at a different level than their underlying indexes. If you're faint of heart or cannot leave your money in them for the long haul they should be avoided. Although investing in index funds is an easy way to invest, it is better to split your capital and invest partly in index funds and partly in managed funds. Studies have shown that diversifying gives better returns and less volatility.

NYSE INDEXES

NYSE indexes closely reflect today's market as NYSE-listed companies account for a substantial portion of the world's economy. Included in these indexes are NYSE-listed U.S. companies which represent 81 percent and 52 percent of the available market capitalization of all publicly traded companies in the United States and around the world, respectively, as of year-end 2007.

The NYSE's objectives in developing proprietary indexes are to showcase the strength of companies listed on the Exchange, and to provide investors and issuers with benchmarks that measure the world's largest marketplace as well as its key segments. The New York Stock Exchange is home to many of the world's most well-established and high-quality companies that meet NYSE's higher listing standards with respect to profitability and company size.

Powered by NYSE MarkeTrac | as of **17:06 ET 08 Feb 2008**

Indexes	Value	Change	% Change
NYSE Composite	8,823.12	-35.92	0.41 %
NYSE Energy	13,279.73	+170.08	1.30 %
NYSE Financial	7,464.53	-133.17	1.75 %
NYSE Health Care	6,567.55	-69.46	1.05 %
NYSE International 100	6,526.22	-18.84	0.29 %
NYSE TMT	6,328.54	+4.07	0.06 %
NYSE US 100	6,441.65	-40.70	0.63 %
NYSE World Leaders	6,581.47	-31.44	0.48 %
NYSE Arca Tech 100	839.37	+6.08	0.73 %

PERFORMANCE MATRIX OF NYSE INDEXES

PERFORMANCE	YTD	1 yr	3 yrs	5 yrs	Volat
NYSE U.S. 100	7.4%	15.4%	9.3%	10.6%	10.7%

PERFORMANCE MATRIX OF NYSE INDEXES					
NYSE International 100	12.6%	23.7%	18.5%	18.8%	12.9%
NYSE TMT	12.7%	25.6%	14.2%	16.3%	18.3%
NYSE World Leaders	9.7%	19.0%	13.1%	13.9%	11.2%
NYSE Composite	9.2%	19.2%	14.6%	15.5%	10.7%
NYSE Financial	-3.5%	4.4%	10.4%	13.7%	8.5%
NYSE Energy	23.6%	39.6%	25.4%	25.0%	15.5%
NYSE Healthcare	4.0%	4.5%	6.9%	8.3%	7.7%
NYSE ARCA Tech 100	11.1%	18.4%	12.1%	19.2%	18.4%

All return numbers are annualized.

*Annualized volatility based on monthly returns over the last five years.

The NYSE indexes are available to be licensed as the basis for tradable products, including exchange-traded funds (ETFs), to be launched in the future.

RELATED INFORMATION
NYSE Euronext Announces 2007 Returns for NYSE Indexes
ETF and Indexes Contact

New York Stock Exchange®, NYSE®, NYSE Composite Index®, NYSE TMT Index®, NYSE Energy Index®, NYSE Financial Index® and NYSE Health Care Index® are registered trademarks and service marks of New York Stock Exchange, Inc.; NYSE U.S. 100 IndexSM, NYSE International 100 IndexSM, NYSE World Leaders IndexSM, and Track the MarketSM are service marks of New York Stock Exchange, Inc. The NYSE U.S. 100 Index, NYSE International 100 Index, NYSE World Leaders Index, and NYSE TMT Index (the "Indexes") are calculated and maintained by Dow Jones Indexes. The Industry Classification Benchmark is proprietary to FTSE International Limited and Dow Jones & Company, Inc. and has been licensed for use. The Indexes and all other information provided by New York Stock Exchange, Inc. ("NYSE"), its affiliates, officers, directors, employees, agents, representatives and third party providers of information and calculation services (the "NYSE Parties") in connection with the Index (collectively "Data") are presented "as is" and without representations or warranties of any kind. The NYSE parties shall not be liable for loss or damage, direct, indirect or consequential, arising from any use of the Data or action taken in reliance upon the Data. Nothing herein constitutes investment, tax, legal or other professional advice, and the NYSE Parties do not recommend the purchase or sale of any particular security or investment. No person may use the Indexes, any of the Data, or any trademark of NYSE in connection with the issuance, trading, marketing or promotion of investment products (e.g., derivatives, structured products, investment funds or investment portfolios) where the price, return and/ or performance of the investment product is based on or related to the Index, without a separate written agreement with NYSE.

www.nyse.com

ANNUITIES AND STOCKS

Are annuities becoming a thing of the past? Billions of dollars have been put into variable annuities but is that the best place to put your money. Insurance companies think so since hefty commissions can be made with the sale of annuities. Are they a good place to stash money for a tax shelter? Where do you go to find an excellent variable annuity? With IRA and 401(k) plans becoming more popular after 2001 legislation, allowing individuals to increase their contributions annuities have become less popular. If you think you might be interested in investing an annuity the following are some things you need to know.

A variable annuity is part mutual fund and part insurance policy. The mutual fund is called a "sub account" and its rate of return gives rise to the term variable. Individuals invest during their working years and usually make withdrawals after retirement. A desirable variable annuity will go with funds that have a wide choice (bonds, both growth and value stocks, foreign markets and large and small companies). The advantages of variable annuities are: upon your death your heirs will receive your initial investment, less your withdrawals; you can postpone paying taxes on your contributions until you begin to withdraw; you can move money from fund to fund without paying taxes as long as the funds are in your sub account.; you may transfer money from one annuity to another without paying tax; you can invest as much money each year as you like. IRA's and 401(k)'s have contribution caps and withdrawals must be started after becoming 70 1.2 years of age. Most variable annuities can be withdrawal free until you reach the age of 85.

Some of the drawbacks of variable annuities are that your profits are taxed at your income tax rate. If it is fairly high you will lose a substantial part of your profit. If you invest in a mutual fund but not in an annuity your capital gains tax is a maximum 20 percent. Most studies comparing the two types of investments favor regular mutual fund investment. Your after-tax return needs to be in an annuity for 20 or more years to come out ahead (not good for people in their fifties or older). Variable annuity fees are higher than regular fees for mutual funds. If you invest in an annuity and change your mind you will usually pay a surrender fee during the first 6 to 8 years for taking part or all of your money out. If you have maxed out your 401(k) and IRA for the year, then you might consider a variable annuity.

WEB SITES

www.variableannuityonline.com

www.annuitynet.com

www.morningstar.com

Another form of annuity is called immediate annuity and are made for people who are retired and want a monthly amount of money to be collected. The investor deposits cash, monthly checks are sent and they never stop. If you live a long time you may get checks even though your initial deposit is gone. The investor may choose between variable and fixed type of annuity. With a fixed immediate annuity you will receive money based on a guaranteed set rate of return, variable immediate annuity depends on the fluctuation of the stock market but you are guaranteed not to lose your initial investment. Immediate annuities may not be a good investment if your heirs are counting on inheriting money as there is no death benefit option. However you can use these options - joint and life survivor (if one spouse dies the other will receive smaller checks until they die); life annuity with period certain (if the investor dies prior to a certain period, five to 20 years, a designated beneficiary will receive the money.

REAL ESTATE INVESTMENT TRUSTS

REITS are investment pools that allow at least 100 shareholders to invest in stock, further diversifying portfolios having equal shares between everyone. They are similar to mutual funds. What makes REITS unique is that anyone can invest in a piece of the commercial real estate pie, the same way they would in the stock market. Pension funds slice up the entire portfolios into pieces of pie and real estate accounts for one slice. Typically, most United State pension funds have a target benchmark of 8 percent for the real estate niche. Investments include shares of loans and other credit obligations or real estate collateral. This type of investment is highly attractive due to liquidity. A reputation surrounds REITS, as they typically increase your total return while lowering overall risk. Inflations rates are outpaced by dividend growth rates. Long-term gains and share price appreciation can be beneficial to the portfolios exposed to liquidity (stock markets) while having low leverage, having the potential do have a nice cash flow.

One pro of REITS is that the income streams are predictable. When an investment is made to a commercial real estate property, whether it be office, residential, hotel, industrial, or retail, rents can be counted on, as leases are long-term, making the investment a little more predictable. This also includes storage centers, warehouses, and all types of lodging facilities, healthcare facilities, and natural resources.

This type of investment has proven to be profitable for the majority of pension funds, who hire the right advisors who have excellent records of accomplishment. Some pension funds do directly invest in real estate and they usually do not have an advisor assisting them. There are many choices out there for REITS. REITS are also publicly traded, with individuals owning shares of the property. REITS purchase either actual real estate assets, or mortgages that provide financing for homes. Hybrid REITS are a combination of the two. Cash flow comes from the returns of the mortgages. Dividend yields tend to be higher than that of a stock for a REIT.

Another advantage of REITS is tax considerations, which again produce a higher yield. It distributes 90 percent of its taxable income on an annual basis to shareholders, but shareholders do have to pay taxes on dividends gained. REIT investment decisions are made on behalf of a board of directors or trustees. From 1971 to 2006, REITS have outperformed the U.S. benchmarks. In the year 2006, apartment and office REITS were the most highly favored, while manufactured housing, specialty, and mixed-use properties were the least favored.

A good place to start is with the National Association of Real Estate Investment Trusts. NAREIT offers many services for investors, keeping them informed on the latest on U.S. REITS and publicly traded real estate companies worldwide. The Web site (**www.nareit.com**) allows those on the market to network among themselves. The investors can find out what REITS are available on which index, with frequently asked questions, as well as specific REIT data, updated regularly. Analysis is made by NAREIT on the top REITS in each cap range by gold, silver, and bronze. Information of this sort can be found under the press releases.

THE THREE REIT AMIGOS

NAREIT explains that within the REIT world, there are three types of REITS – publicly exchanged, private, and non-exchange traded. Publicly exchanged are those shares that do trade on the national stock exchange, and that are traded on a daily basis with minimum liquidity standards; there are over 200 choices. NAREIT provides all of the stock exchange listings divided by each channel. Brokers can make anywhere from $20 to $150 on one single trade, while investment banks receive an investment fee of 2 percent to 7 percent in underwriting fees and follow-on offerings, which are based on the deal size. The minimum investment amount is one share. Because it is under SEC jurisdiction, many reports are made available to the public.

In non-exchange matters, REITS still have to file with the SEC, but they do not trade on national stock exchanges. Depending on the company, redemption programs are limited and the holding period for required liquidation is ten years. A share of this kind begins at $1000 to $2500. Both of these REITS have directors – with publicly exchanged REITS, directors are chosen, while non-exchange is directed by the North American Securities Administration Association (NASAA) where there is a board consisting of independent directors. Non-exchange has the same requirements under the SEC as non-exchanged REITS do. Private REITS are another story. They are not protected by the SEC, nor do they trade on national stock exchanges. Redemption is limited by most companies, and broker commissions vary. This type is really meant for high net worth individuals, or institutional investors such as a pension funds that can spend either $1,000 or $25,000 if they wish. In any case, the investors get to re-elect the directors. The REITS have no disclosure obligation or performance measurement in addition to corporate governance, (**http://www.investinreits.com/waystoinvest/comparison.pdf**). In a later chapter, you will have sources in helping you research the best routes.

CASE STUDY: RON KUYKENDALL

National Association of Real Estate Investment Trusts

1875 I Street, NW, Suite 600, Washington, D.C. 20006-5413

Phone: 202-739-9400, Fax: 202-739-9401

www.nareit.com, www.investinreits.com

The average return on all REITS is 34 percent, which is excellent. Generally, REITS compare similarly to that of stocks and bonds, as they have a low correlation among comparison. Since 1972, REITS have outperformed stocks and bonds and have received a lot of attention. A stock-market crash in 2007 scared many investors and they scattered, pulling their investments out of REITS, even when it was not necessary. The average investor knows that he or she has invested in real estate, but what they do not know, in some cases, is whether they have invested in commercial real estate or REITS that invest in mortgages, starting a panic that is almost like a domino effect. Asidefrom this, the only other time REITS were not

CASE STUDY: RON KUYKENDALL

favored was during the dot.com bubble. In the 1970's the S&P 500 index was floating to all time highs and many lost focus on REITS, but this soon came back. At this time, investors were attracted to the technology stocks and bonds. The effect from this lasted about two years from 1998-1999. The best advice from Brad Case, room for REIT allocations domestic or abroad. Kuykendall's investment vice president of research and industry information at NAREIT, is to look at three things when make an investment; 1) Look for those REITS that have performed strong. 2) Look for those REITS that have "reasonable" volatility and 3) Look for those in which there is low correlation as this is the key to diversification. While REITS receive the most attention from institutional investors, individuals are still plugging away too at specific REITS. In most cases, this happens when an individual is educated through a REIT ETF or a mutual fund in which there are REITS involved. Typically, it is the bigger institutional investors that serve as the primary audience for REITS. However, more and more 401(k) plans are allocating to REITS for diversification — the most important factor for investments. Ron Kuykendall, vice president of communications, explains that pension systems are continuously making observation plays on the fact that, in the past fiveyears, individual investors and their 401(k) accounts have quadrupled in the past five years, all the more reason the plans are making REITS adjustments. For some 401(k) plans options are being cut back, but a long-term trend is such that the REIT options are increasing for both institutional and individual investors.

This is a slow process, however. Examples include the California Public Employees' Retirement System and kid-sister California State Teachers' Retirement System, the largest pension systems in the United States. In 2007, these pension funds have been readjusting the real estate portfolios accommodating REITS. As of November 2007, CalPERS has considered adopting up to 30 percent of its real estate portfolio specific on REITS. While there are hundreds of pension funds in this world, a few domestic and mentionable funds in this phenomenal trend include the Alaska Permanent Fund, Oregon Public Employees Retirement System, and Orange County Public Employee Retirement System. For pension plans, there are at least three good reasons to invest in REITS Kuykendall explains 1)The investment is an excellent diversifier in a portfolio, 2) It

CASE STUDY: RON KUYKENDALL

offers hedge against inflation and 3) Global opportunities are an emerging and popular trend at this time, offering even more diversification.

"Some stock market investment provide risk adjusted returns and some low correlation, but REITS provide both," Brad Case, vice president of research and industry information of NAREIT said.

CHAPTER 2

How To Invest

Decision, Decisions...Decisions. Just as there are many investment choices, there are also many choices in determining how you want to place an order among buying or selling your stock securities — this is trading. Someone somewhere suggested "paper trading." This is a good practice tool for those who wish to learn as much as possible as an individual investor. As a newcomer, you can make observations of the stocks in comparison while making notes and/or fake investments. The goal would be to see if you are comfortable enough with the market, and if you know how to play the game.

In reality, you can place a market order, day order, stop order, stop-limit order, and good-til-cancelled order. By becoming familiar with the choices, transactions can be made smoother and more predictable. Again, it is up to you to hire a broker, or you can trade independently online. You must specifically tell the broker what it is you want when buying or selling stock.

The first step is deciding which way to go on a trade. At this point, you should feel confident about what the different options are. To begin a trade, the buyer and seller first agree on the value of the investment. The money then goes from one hand to another. The actual trade begins with exchange floors and electronics. The exchange floor is the floor of a market, such as that of the New York Stock Exchange (see Chapter 3). What takes place on an exchange floor is first your broker sends your request to this so called "floor" in which the clerk finds an offer that matches your request. A floor trader is familiar with the process and should know where to be at the right time to fulfill your order. When the clerk and the trader can make a deal, your broker will then notify you with a final agreed-upon price. This is followed by confirmation. If there is a disagreement about the value of a stock the price can fluctuate, with a possibility to make more money. A tick is the smallest measurement increment of price change allowed by an exchange, and the sizes of change vary. With stocks, it was an eighth of a dollar, then in 1997 reduced to sixteenths and in 2001 reduced again to one-one hundredth of a dollar. These days however, almost all stocks, bonds, and commodities are no longer counted by things such as 1/8th of a point, and are instead tracked by dollars and cents. Those who are keeping a focus on market trends keep an eye on ticks. It is not relevant in evaluating a company's growth potential, but ticks are what makes the buyers and sellers move in and out of stocks. An alpha is the measure of a stock's price movements. This is caused by company decisions. Beta is what measures performance in response to the entire stock market or changes in the economy and adjusted interest rates. Alpha examines the stock by eliminating market fluctuations. It is as if securities changed on their own merits, which include earnings per share, labor relations, and management. In regards to a mutual fund, alpha represents the relationship of the funds performance to its beta. To calculate a historical alpha, you need to know a risk-free rate of return, the securities historical background, and the past returns of the market.

All of this can be done electronically as well, making the process even faster. The NASDAQ is electronic, while other systems can vary. In an electronic system, confirmation of sales and purchases is received right away. A bull market is a common term you will hear about the stock market, which means things are looking good; it means prices are rising and the trend is expected to continue. In opposite, a bear market is one in which prices decline.

Market & Limit Orders

Market orders and limit orders are the two most popular investment strategies.

Market orders include buying or selling a stock at its current market price, or the trading price at that particular time. That said, when you have access to real-time quotes, the price you requested should be close to that, if not the same as when the trade request is made. However, the price you pay when your order take place may differ from what was originally quoted by your broker. This is true when you buy a multitude of shares because prices will differ in various parts of the orders, especially when markets are volatile and are rapidly changing. The difference between the buying and the selling price of a stock is a spread.

Limit orders can help in losing a lot among a spread, especially if you have varied stock choices. When there is no spread it is an agency trade, and you are lucky. Infrequent trades tend to have bigger spreads. A fast-moving market portrays bouncy stocks and many recent IPOs. Another thing you should take into consideration is that overall costs of a transaction can vary depending on how you make the investment. There is low commission on a broker's behalf, as there is not too much work involved. It is safer to use high-volume stocks in a market order to avoid large spreads. In any case, your asking price could be higher than the market price, which means you may not gain much.

In solo attributions, always check to make sure there is confirmation after you have placed an order. During a day trade, a confirmation will follow shortly after your request. After hours your order confirmation would be delayed, as your request is in a review process and does not happen right away.

With limit orders, you request a limit in which a security can be bought or sold at that price or lower. In comparison to a market order, this request is not guaranteed. In some cases your request may not be executed because of fluctuations in the market in which that number could quickly be passed. The biggest convenience is that you will not be purchasing anything at too high of a price, and if you are selling it will be sold above the limit price. Another advantage is that you, the investor, can control the length of time that the order is outstanding by limit. Requesting this through your broker is typically more expensive than a market order would be. If an order is conditional the investors can still trade at the limit order price, allowing for more leniency on the investors request. In opposite, a discretionary order allows the broker to buy or sell at his/her convenience at the best looking gain. There are some restrictive terms to this, but the trader will decide on the timing. Selling a limit order is what you are willing to sell your stock for, and this request will take place once that price is hit or higher.

Day Orders

www.otcstockexchange.com

A request to buy or sell stock is a day order. This pertains to a specific day and that day only. Otherwise, such a request turns into an after-hours trade. An order can only take place during a trading session, and if you miss it a new order must be placed for a following trading session. The investor's goal is to move in quickly to make a profit and then leave. The media has a big effect on what is going on among the stocks, because what is reported will make some stocks drop and others jump. Stock symbols look attractive, and so does a good opportunity, so this is how it all begins. There are day trading firms, like the broker, and these people observe in detail daily changes, buying at a lower price and selling at higher prices. The difference is what they make as commission. Some people do this from home while others have actual firms — both use high-tech equipment to keep up with hundreds of scores, watching and waiting to make the right moves at the right times. Other day traders chip in on what seems to be a more permeated stock by observing that it has been rising and will continue to do so. They bail out once any sort of failure appears. Then there are "momentum" investors. These people are message board admirers, chat room attendees, and full-board email readers, and they strive to keep up with any stock information. In chat rooms picks are communicated instantly, which serves faster than a message board. Message boards have proven to be a useful source of information for hard-core investors. While it does not force anyone to make a specific decision, often times the messages posted will influence you to one extreme or another as thousands of people post daily about buying or selling a stock. These boards are also called electronic boards or forums. For the most part, however, the readers peruse boards looking for some valuable information, but just as with anything on the Internet, you cannot always believe what you see. When posting your own message, watch what you say, because often times the message will linger for a while. Proprietary message forums do exist, although many are public.

DAY TRADING SITES	
Company	Web Site
ActiveTrade	www.activetrade.net
All-Tech Investment Group Inc.	www.attain.com
Day Traders On-line	www.daytraders.com

DAY TRADING SITES	
Company	Web Site
Digital Traders	www.trading-place.net
Pristine Day Trader	www.pristine.com

After-Hours Trading

Trading can take place outside of regular trading hours of the major stock exchanges. Some stocks do not give you this advantage. The standard hours are 9:30 to 4:30 East Coast time. In some cases, this sort of desire is more relevant to high net-worth individuals, pension funds, or mutual funds. Through an electronic communications network (ECN), an individual can continue to place orders regardless of what time it is. If an ECN cannot match your request, it will send you elsewhere to another market center. This market can be more volatile and less liquid, bringing greater risk. It is not as easy to convert your stocks. This is due in part to the availability of buyers as sellers, as they are more active during the day. This means less trading volume for certain stocks, resulting in greater price fluctuations. When speaking of risk in this instance, you cannot see or act upon quotes as you would in day trading. Certain firms allow investors to view quotes from a trading system once after-hours are reached. It is your responsibility or your brokers to find out if you can trade among these quotes. At times you cannot complete a trade of this sort. A disadvantage of online investing is computer delays, which can cause a failure in getting your requests executed. An after-hours order can be alive during the regular business hours in some instances.

One of the best things about the Internet is that it is available 24 hours a day. Since the NYSE, for example, is only running up around normal business hours, some people turn to after hours trading. However, those daytime trading sites may have information on the after-hours quotes, including the news. A good place to start with after-hour trading is Harrisdirect and Charles Schwab. There are other sites already mentioned in this book that offer a multitude of information as well. Keep in mind, stocks offer more liquidity in after hours trading as they can be quickly converted to cash. This does not pertain to all stocks though. Hours vary among brokerages and may also have different policies among each after hour club such as cost per limit order for so many shares.

Stop-Loss Orders

Also known as a stop-market order, stop-loss takes place when your security reaches a certain price. It accounts for a loss on your securities positions, and any loss will stop at that limit. Some people use this method when they are unable to keep an eye on their stocks either because they are on vacation or for another reason. It assures that if you are going to lose something, you will not lose more than a specified percentage. It is also known as a sell-stop. Your investment is always below the current market price, and the investor or broker can still sell the stock at the next available price. It advises your broker to sell once it hits this point because you do not want your loss to be any greater. Upon reaching a stop-loss the stock becomes a limit order or market order, which leads us to stop-loss limit orders. This happens when a security is purchased at a specific limit price. A limit order gives the trader control over the price at which the trade is executed, and a stop-loss buy limit order allows for an exchange at the limit price or lower. This takes place when a trader or an investor wants to put a limit on what is spent to buy a stock. With a limit order, there is not too much risk if and when prices rise sharply. When there is a stop-loss sell limit order it is vice versa, and the sale can only take place at the set limit price. If there are not buyers or sellers interested in the execution price then this strategy would not work in your favor. Some people tell the market makers (broker) to either give them what they want in a request or else. Not really, but an All or Nothing order means the same thing. If an order cannot be filled at the price you request, then it is easy to never-mind with an AON. There is also the "Fill or Kill" request. This does not mean the broker will be killed if an order is not filled. It is the same as an AON; the only difference is that the order request is to be filled immediately.

Investment Portfolio

When you have a portfolio, you have a collection of all types of investments, including stocks, bonds, and any other asset. In any portfolio, the point is to diversify with different investment options, which levels out the returns and eliminates risk. Asset allocation means the amount of money you plan to put towards each slice of your pie for whatever investments you choose, it. Those that do not like to lose money are usually the ones that put small amounts in stocks for short time frames, while those who have a few years and are willing to take a risk will sit back and watch with an expectation that will assist in a long-term decision. In preparation for an investment portfolio you should determine what you want from your investments. You should decide first hand if you want long-term or short-term goals and then put them in check. Is the purpose for retirement, college savings, and a boat perhaps? If you can pinpoint a time frame, this would be helpful too. Next, look at your budget. How much can you afford to loose? Or how much will you be allocating and how many times? Your portfolio will really depend upon what kinds of returns you want to achieve. If you have a broker, he/she should advise you in the right decisions as well. Portfolios should be reevaluated annually, therefore, in the end, investment decisions should serve you well. Another plan is to set aside at least 10 percent of your annual salary for investments.

The main purpose of a portfolio is for balance. Spreading the risk of your investments is done through a mix including stocks, bonds, mutual funds, or other vehicles. This helps reduce your risk because if you invest everything you have in one stock you can lose everything you, but if you invest in several stocks the chance that they will all go belly-up at the same time is small.

Good-Til-Cancelled-Order

Exactly as the description says, this is security order to buy or sell at your set price until you decide to cancel it. If a GTC does not apply, the order is canceled at the end of the day in which the order was placed. These orders typically last anywhere from 30 to 90 days before your order expires and is reinstated. When you cancel your order, you need to make certain that your actual request has been made. Because the "speed of online trading can be deceptive," you should know that your broker is the primary person who submits your request to the market, as you cannot do it yourself (Grey 123). This is not necessarily a sufficient thing to do with regards to quick trading in a market order.

CHAPTER 3

Stock Markets & Things

THE NEW YORK STOCK EXCHANGE

www.nyse.com

The story goes something like this: In the late 1700s a group of brokers met under a tree in Manhattan as if they were getting ready to play a game of poker. It was during this time when the first trading of securities is said to have taken place. History does tend to repeat itself, and certainly even those that are not investors have heard of a stock market, the New York Stock Exchange – and we should know what it is since it has been around since 1817. Then, known as the New York Stock and Exchange Board, NYSE was adopted in 1863, giving individuals plenty of time to become familiar with investments.

The stock market opened on Wall Street in 1965, but, in all actuality, the federal government started the market with loans as far back as 1790, paying debt during the American Revolutionary War against Great Britain. Wall Street is actually derived from a group of people out of New Amsterdam, now known as New York City, known as 'De Waal Straat." These Dutch explorers where known as Walloons.

The street, which sits in lower Manhattan, in none other than New York, of course, is the first home of the NYSE. Instead of a building, the term Wall Street accounts for the surrounding neighborhood around this building. In short, Wall Street is the headquarters for the major stock exchange players covered in this chapter. The NYSE is by far the largest stock exchange in the world by investments (dollars) with nearly 3,000 stock choices, whether it is debt, securities, binds, stocks, or other options. These securities may or may not be registered. This is the only source that uses floor traders; the rest of the markets are computer drive. Its primary duty is to oversee member transfers and applicants while supervising member activities. The exchange sets policies and lists securities, in addition to updating members monthly on any disciplinary actions made against a brokerage. The Web site is able to pull up all pertinent information on brokers and brokerages in addition to years and background information. After a broker communicates with a specialist on the exchange floor, sellers are researched on one of at least nine ECNs that match your request.

In the world of NASDAQ, the broker researches the trading screen in which shares are listed by how many are available and at what price. An electronic message is sent to a market maker once these goals are met, at which point the shares are purchased.

NASDAQ is recognized as a "dealer market" where as the NYSE is called the "auction market." As brokers earn commission serving as an agent for its customers, this is called an agency market. The dealer market of NASDAQ proves different, as deals are made electronically. Companies interested in this medium must "have a minimum of $1.1 million shares publicly held, 2,000 shareholders of 100 shares, and $40 million in market capitalization." (Price, 152).

NATIONAL ASSOCIATION OF SECURITIES DEALERS AUTOMATED QUOTATIONS

www.nasdaq.com

The biggest of the index choices is NASDAQ, serving as the largest ECN trading place in the United States. There are over 3,000 companies that trade more OTC shares on a daily basis. On the first trading day, this number was at 2,500. In 1971 the National Association of Securities Dealers (compromised of anyone in the industry in the U.S.) founded the market, which is monitored by the Securities and Exchange Commission. The purpose is to oversee the activity of several brokerage firms while regulating trades of equities, securities, bonds, and more, in addition to overseeing thousands of registered security representatives. In 1998, NASDAQ merged with the American Stock Exchange. This move made it the largest, as a combined 15,000 companies were listed.

Companies interested possess at least 500,000 shares with a market capitalization of over $3 million. There is not a physical location like the NYSE for NASDAQ. As mentioned in chapter one, the OTC market are cheaper stocks that are traded frequently. They are traded on pink sheets, which make accurate pricing difficult. The exchange trades over 1.8 billion shares per day, and current financial information is displayed 24 hours per day on a large electronic board in New York's Times Square. In qualifying to be promoted by NASDAQ, a company must have a stock price of $1 while the total price of outstanding stocks should be over $1.1 million. Those who cannot qualify still fit in NASDAQ's small cap category. Trading with NASDAQ is cheaper that the NYSE, making stocks more volatile.

Originally it was just the NASDAQ market until the mid 1980s when the smaller companies were divided by the larger. This is when the small cap category came along. The initial intentions of NASDAQ were to increase the OTC opportunities, as many stocks were unable to meet that that was required of the NYSE.

AMERICAN STOCK EXCHANGE

www.amex.com

Introducing the third largest stock exchange market in the United States, the American Stock Exchange is located in New York City. It represents about 10 percent of domestic securities. It is actually merged with NASDAQ, but it focuses more on small-cap opportunities (typically market capitalization in the range of $300 million to $2 billion but dependent upon the broker), exchange-traded funds, and derivatives. This is where stock index securities were first created. That said, you can buy interests in all stocks such as "Standard & Poor's 500, the 30 stocks of the Dow Jones Industrial Average, or the NASDAQ 100." (Gray, Menke 290). Index securities are essentially the same as stocks, as they trade easily during the day with high liquidity.

S&P 500

www.standardandpoor.com

The S&P 500 serves primarily as the mutual fund gauge. It is an index that has the large-cap stocks in which 500 companies are involved and most are domestic. It observes what is happening among the NYSE, AMEX, and NASDAQ. McGraw-Hill is the backbone of Standard & Poor, an advisory firm among other things. In existence, there are S&P Global 1200 and 1500 indices. Global 1200 consist of global stock options of S&P including 31 countries, and 1500 is all U.S. stocks composed by S&P's indexes. This includes both stocks and mutual funds. Stocks in the index are those that can trade on the NYSE or NASDAQ, and companies involved are large. Mutual funds or index funds tend to replicate the S&P 500, as it serves as a model for the financial market. Managers of mutual funds will have the same stocks and proportions in an effort to duplicate gaining the same performance.

In comparing your portfolio with the rest of the market, you will learn whether your stock over performed, underperformed, or just did not do much of anything. Again, its purpose is mostly for those large-cap investors.

DOW JONES

www.dj.com

Reporters in the late 1800s founded Dow Jones, a well-respected financial firm. Two of the reporter's last names were Dow and Jones. The third one's last name must have been too long, it was Bergstresser. There were 12 stocks in 1886 and by 1928 a shift from 20 stocks went to 30. The company is privately owned, but publicly traded. The company has several indices ranging from hedge fund indexes to composite averages, making it the most observed. By the way, an indices is a just an index of stocks. A Wilshire 5000 serves as a market capitalization weighted index providing the market value of all stocks that trade in the U.S., including limited partnerships, stocks, REITS, and others which trade on AMEX/NASDAQ and the NYSE. All stocks are publicly traded (for the general public or government owned) for those in the stock exchange world.

Examples of stocks include American Express, Citgroup, General Electric, Home Depot, Microsoft, McDonald's, Procter & Gamble, and Wal-Mart.

RUSSELL INDEX

www.russell.com/indexes

An index that tracks market segments on a worldwide basis is the Russell index, which has management in either mutual funds or exchange traded funds (open-ended investment companies that trade all day). ETFs tend to mock that of the stock market indexes like the S&P. The index holds most of its weight with the help of institutional investors, and by mid 2007 the U.S. had over $4 trillion in assets. Within the index, there are both value and growth stocks. Starting with Russell 3000, this index includes capitalization companies large and small in the U.S. Market. The 1000 index is consistent with the top 1000 large-cap stocks from the 3000 index, while the 2000 index contains the small-caps, which are at the bottom of the 3000 index. Likewise, Russell also has a top 200 index (mega-cap, largest stocks) and a top 50 index (performance of top 50 companies). The list goes on for observations in mid- to small-cap, as well as an index that includes those that cannot be found on the S&P 500. The company manages over $230 billion worldwide and has had a reputation since 1936.

SEC REGISTERED STOCK EXCHANGES	
American Stock Exchange	www.amex.com
Boston Stock Exchange	www.bostonstock.com
Chicago Board Options Exchange	www.cboe.com
Chicago Stock Exchange	www.chx.com
International Securities Exchange	www.iseoptions.com
Philadelphia Stock Exchange	www.phlx.com

SEC REGISTERED STOCK EXCHANGES	
Nasdaq Stock Market LLC	www.nasdaq.com
National Stock Exchange (once Cincinnati Stock Exchange)	www.nsx.com
NYSE Arca, Inc. (once Pacific Exchange)	www.nysearca.com
New York Stock Exchange	www.nyse.com

FOREIGN EXCHANGE MARKETS

Now that you are familiar with the NYSE and NASDAQ, there are a number of foreign markets to be considered. In 1995 the Federation of Euro-Asian Stock Exchanges (FEAS) was started with 12 members, now there are more than 30. Emerging stock exchanges in Asia and Europe are eligible to join. The governing body meets once a year and is comprised of all members. Twelve of the members make up the Executive Committee. Shortly after formation a mission was adopted to help development of member markets and facilitate securities trading among members.NYSE Euronext, the holding company created by the combination of NYSE Group, Inc. and Euronext N.V., was launched on April 4, 2007. NYSE Euronext (NYSE/New York and Euronext/Paris: NYX) operates the world's largest and most liquid exchange group and offers the most diverse array of financial products and services. NYSE Euronext, which brings together six cash equities exchanges in five countries and six derivatives exchanges, is a world leader for listings, trading in cash equities, equity and interest rate derivatives, bonds and the distribution of market data.

A goal of Euronext was to help small and midsized companies become able to be on the stock market in the Euro zone. Alternext was created as a program, which started with a single list (Eurolist by Euronext). Alternext provides new investment opportunities to investors and is dedicated to ensuring their security and protection. Companies in many sectors list with Alternext because of the operating methods and listing requirements that companies feel will help them attain their goals.

Alternative Investment Market (AIM) is operated by the London Stock Exchange and came into being in 1995 replacing the Unlisted Securities Market (USM). Companies that list with AIM have an opportunity to establish their shares' market value, have a trading exchange and raise expansion capital. AIM has around 400 companies listed with a wide variety of market cap index. Investing in AIM companies gives a tax advantage as they are listed as "unquoted investments" and each year an investor holds AIM shares there is a 5 percent "taper relief" on gains purchased after 4/6/2000.

A study done in 2006 by M&A Boutique Innovation Advisors showed that small US technology companies are accepting risk by listing on AIM. The study also claims that, after two years of going public, stock may be worth less than half on the initial IPO. Research showed that after two years, NASDAQ companies gained 12 percent, AIM companies lost 57 percent. Research for years three through five also showed NASDAQ values to be better than AIM. An AIM response said that its unique market makes a study of comparison of other markets difficult.

A study done in 2007 by the London School of Economics and Political Science found the following: AIM's competitive strength is due partly to location and partly due to the regulatory system; since the dot.com boom collapse AIM is attracting a wide range of investors; companies joining AIM after 2000, on average, have given investors better returns than the wider market; less than 3 percent of listed companies, in the last four years, have failed even though most companies are new or operate in high-risk ventures; and amount of capital raised in the last few years has increased dramatically.

A London stock exchange, started in 2004, is PLUS Markets Group, trading securities such as the FTSE 100 and AIM and PLUS unlisted shares. It uses trade reporting and independent price formation as its trading platform. "PLUS-quoted" has over 200 small and mid-cap companies and offers an alternative for using AIM. A goal of PLUS is to have applicants of higher quality than some other exchanges. It has been recognized by the Financial Services Authority and given Recognised Investment Exchange status with competitive cash equity exchange.

NEWSPAPERS & THE INTERNET

In all actuality, newspaper readership has been declining for decades. The Internet does not help the situation, but there are a few good newspapers out there, such as USA Today, Wall Street Journal. Both papers will keep you up-to-date on stock numbers whether you are at a bagel shop, having your car washed, or are in your break room at work. The Wall Street Journal was created in 1884 when the Dow

Jones and Company's newsletter, *Customer's Afternoon Letter*, was converted.

For stock information, newspapers are just as convenient as the Internet. But for the high-speed Internet fans, ubiquitous information can also be at your fingertips in seconds. There are all kinds of financial newsletters online. Often people can register for to receive free newsletters, but there are some that have paid subscriptions. Perhaps the most well-recognized online magazines are *Forbes and Fortune*. Online information is more up-to-date, as information can be updated constantly while print opportunities are not that giving, and lag a little bit behind on the latest news. Most financial Web sites assist with financial decisions, planning, stock quotes, and more. For example, the newspaper *Wall Street Journal* has a Web site that offers portfolio management, the latest on news, stock information, and many other accommodating options for the investor. This Web site can also provide you with the latest news via e-mail. The next hottest is The *New York Times*, which also has a lot to offer.

While all Web sites may seem the same, each site offers something different such as

The Dallas Morning News. It is a good source to become familiar with, as it some information that other sources may not, such as treasury bonds.

NEWSPAPER, NEWS AND MAGAZINE WEB SITES:	
interactive.wsj.com	Wall Street Journal
www.nytimes.com	New York Times
www.barrons.com	Barron's Online

NEWSPAPER, NEWS AND MAGAZINE WEB SITES:	
www.smartmoney.com	SmartMoney.com
ww.washingtonpost.com	Washington Post
dallasnews.com	Dallas Morning News
latimes.com/business/erporter/ etrading	Los Angeles Times
www.forbes.com	Forbes Magazine
www.bloomberg.com	Bloomberg Personal Finance
www.cbs.marketwatch.com	CBS MarketWatch
www.investors.com	Investor's Business Daily
www.businessweek.com	Business Week Online
www.economist.com	Economist.com
www.abcnews.go.com	ABC Stockmarket Broadcasts
www.businesstalkradio.net	Business Talk Radio Network

CASE STUDY: NANCY WEBMAN

Pensions & Investments Online

711 Third Avenue

New York, NY 10017

www.pionline.com

Nancy Webman- Editor

nwebman@pionline.com

(212) 210-0100 – voice

(212) 210-0117 – fax

In reference to an excellent online source, Pensions&Investments Online offers great information for the investor on many different levels. All of the information comes from trained writers in which real estate and investing is covered, including national pension systems. What makes the

CASE STUDY: NANCY WEBMAN

company is unique is such that miscellaneous surveys are conducted on a regular basis, offering a resource that many publications do not have. Data may include a collection of the largest money managers, top 100 pension funds, real estate investment managers, in addition to fixed income roundtables, while advising the readers of future surveys. The company provides original information in which they can manipulate everything in a way that will assist readers and investors'. The system keeps an archive of information and once a year, a databook is published of highlights thought the year plus extras. This book offers things that maybe did not make the cut for the site, but was good enough to be published. The best thing about this site is that news caters to all kinds including hedge funds, endowments private equity, trading, real estate and so on. The writers dig for information that would not be available elsewhere. Since business tends to keep up with technology, P&I offers blog banks, Webcast, conferences, and calendars. Investment tools are always important and for those media fund gurus, Lipper's Web Solution is recom-mended in addition to Popular Index Portfolio Opportunity Distributions. Investors can work with PIPODS to keep track of investment portfolios while measuring the performance of a manager. First and foremost with the web site is the latest information on the stock indexes as well as the news, covering all niches. P&I will be revamping the web site. Material is available free-of-charge today, but at some point the web site will charge a subscription. The site is available to whoever wishes to use it. However, seemingly the average pension fund describes the reader as well as the executives who manage the flow of funds. Foundations and individuals count, too.

EXAMPLE

"NYSE EURONEXT TO BUY AMEX"

Posted: **January 17, 2008**, 5:57 PM EST

NYSE Euronext announced today that it would acquire the American Stock Exchange for $260 million in common stock under an agreement approved by boards of both *companies. The deal which still needs regulatory approval and approval from Amex members is expected to close in the third quarter, according to an NYSE Euronext news release. NYSE Euronext expects to save $100 million a year in cost savings, including relocating Amex to the NYSE trading floor."*

EX. 2

"STOCKS CONTINUE TO FALL; BERNANKE BACKS STIMULUS"

Posted: January 17, 2008, 2:56 PM EST

"U.S. stocks fell sharply today on further evidence the economy is slowing down, even as Federal Reserve Chairman Ben Bernanke called for quick fiscal stimulus and decisive moves on the interest-rate front.

The Dow Jones industrial average closed down 306.95, or 2.46 percent, at 12,159.21; the index has given up more than 1,100 points — a loss of 8.3 percent — since closing 2007 at 13,264.82 points. The S&P 500 fell 39.95, or 2.91%, ending at 1,333.25; and the NASDAQ composite closed down 47.69, or 1.99 percent, at 2,346.90. All numbers are preliminary..."

TODAY'S MARKETS...DJ INDUSTRIAL			
DJ Industrial	NASDAQ	S&P 500	RUSS2KG
DJ Industrial RT	12063.78	-95.43	(- 0.78%)
NASDAQ	2341.58	-7.87	(- 0.33%)
S&P 500	1324.48	-9.36	(- 0.70%)
RUSS2KG	368.30	-4.08	(- 1.10%)

P&I distributes news via email on a daily basis for professionals regarding request for proposals demotions, promotions, and so forth. The company launches in 1973. The international newspaper of money management has proven to be a success as the web site offers more than enough information providing coverage for an audience of all kinds. Reporters surface worldwide with curiosity, professionalized in specific topics. Other topics covered include global investment strategies or changes, technology, legislative reports, product development and corporate governance.

EX. 3

(Survey provided by Pension and Investments)

BIGGEST REAL ESTATE INVESTMENT TRUSTS (2007)	
Ranked by equity market capitalization of institutional shareholders, dollars in millions.	
Firm	Assets
Simon Property Group	$19,717
ProLogis	$14,155
General Growth Properties	$13,004
Archstone-Smith	$12,623
Boston Properties	$12,300
Equity Residential	$12,213
Host Hotels & Resorts	$11,875
Public Storage	$8,500
SL Green Realty	$7,680
Macerich	$7,121
TOTAL	$119,188

EXAMPLE

MKS INSTRUMENTS JUMPS ON Q4 EARNINGS NEWS AND Q1 EPS GUIDANCE [MKSI]

2/7/2008 9:28:10 AM (corrects quarter in headline to Q4 from Q5)

"MKS Instruments (MKSI) rose in pre-market trading, up nearly 7 percent. The advance came as the company reported its fourth-quarter earnings and set its first-quarter outlook. Shares were up $1.22 around 9:20 am ET, climbing to $19.11. If pre-market gains hold, the stock will take back Wednesday's losses. MKS Instruments posted fourth-quarter net income of $15.2 million or $0.27 per share, compared to $26.5 million or $0.47 per share in the prior year quarter.Non-GAAP net income for the quarter totaled $18.6 million or $0.33 per share, compared to $25.9 million or $0.46 per share in the fourth-quarter of 2006.

Sales for the quarter were $184.1 million, down 8 percent from previous year's sales of $199.9 million. On average, analysts polled by First Call/Thomson Financial expected the company to earn $0.25 per share on revenues of $169.75 million for the quarter. Looking ahead, the company expects first quarter earnings to be in the range of $0.24 - $0.31 per share, non-GAAP earnings in the range of $0.28 - $0.35 per share. First-quarter sales were projected to range between $180 million and $190 million. Wall Street analysts have a consensus earnings estimate of $0.26 per share on revenues of $173.33 million for the first-quarter."

STOCKS MAY SEE MORE WEAKNESS EVEN AS VOLATILE TREND CONTINUES

"The major U.S. index futures are pointing to a lower opening on Thursday. Stocks may remain on the defensive given the incremental negative tidings in the form of a smaller than expected drop in jobless claims, anemic retail sales reported for January by the nation's retailers and bleak guidance issued by networking giant Cisco Systems (CSCO). The lean patch is expected to continue in the days to come until the markets begin to see some signals of a rebound in growth. That said, one should not be surprised to see an occasional buying surge, as traders move to take advantage of the volatility. After seeing strength for the better part of the session on Wednesday, the major averages gave back some ground in the last two hours of trading. The optimism seen in the morning was built on the back of better-than-expected productivity growth and some positive earnings reports. However, underlying fears of a potential recession overrode the positive sentiment, triggering a sell-off. The Dow Industrials fell 65.03 points or 0.53 percent to 12,200 and the NASDAQ Composite was off 30.82 points or 1.33 percent to 2,279. Meanwhile, the S&P 500 Index receded 10.19 points or 0.76 percent to 1,327. Disney (DIS) lent support to the Dow, with a 4.76 percent move to the upside following its solid fourth quarter results. However, AIG (AIG), Boeing (BA), General Motors (GM), Home Depot (HD), Hewlett-Packard (HPQ), Intel (INTC), Microsoft (MSFT), AT&T (T) and Wal-Mart Stores (WMT) saw significant weakness. Most sectors witnessed selling, with the exception of gold and airline stocks. Other transportation stocks also saw modest buying interest.

Technical analysis of the Dow Industrials suggests that a downtrend is firmly in place. Both the 50-day and 21-day moving averages are trending lower, and the index is trading below these two averages. The average remains poised to test its January lows. Nevertheless, the momentum indicator of the relative strength index is rising modestly from oversold levels, suggesting the potential for an uptrend. The Dow is trading close to a support level around 12,050. A violation of this level could push the average to its next support level around 11,650. Apart from these levels, the index also has support around the 10,950 level. On the upside, the key levels to watch out for are 12,800, 13,180 and 13,230. The Labor Department's productivity report showed that non-farm business productivity rose at a better than expected annualized pace of 1.8 percent in the fourth quarter. Nevertheless, the increase trailed the 6 percent increase in the third quarter. The drop was mainly due to a 1.5 percent decline in number of hours worked, as self-employment declined. In a public speech on Wednesday, Philadelphia Fed President Charles Plosser said the Fed's aggressive interest rate cuts were appropriate. Plosser is of the view that slowing growth may not curtail inflation and he expects growth to trend between 1 percent and 2 percent in 2008. Plosser estimates an inflation rate of around 2-2.5 percent for 2008. The Fed President confessed that there are early signals of weakening of the Fed's credibility. Developments on the political front were also responsible for the bearish sentiment in the markets. Cantor economists see the lead that Republican candidate John McCain has built over other candidates as a negative development for the markets, as McCain is considered to be weak on the economy. Meanwhile, the close contest witnessed in the Democratic camp is also worrying traders."

CHAPTER 4

Research and Tools

S ometimes people are just challenged. This comes into play with Web sites as a good Web master must provide at least three navigation systems per Web page to meet the needs of the reader. This is because everyone has different tastes and different ways of doing things. Many financial Web sites are helpful, but a good search engine will assist in this process as well. Yahoo, Ta-dah, **altavista.com**, **excite.com**, **infoseek.com**, **dogpile. com**, and **google.com** can all be good sources of financial information. The many choices offer something for every person out there. Something as simple as your bookmark or favorites option within your Web browser becomes very useful for many. If you plan to become a regular observer, you should make checking information on the Web a habit.

Some people may say everyone knows about **Yahoo.com** and all the other search engines, but you would be surprised at how many are not familiar with advanced research and quick tidbits about the Internet.

THE BASICS OF THE INTERNET

Since the subject is "online" the investor should feel comfortable at any web site where the navigation is beneficial yet simplified. All Web sites should provide a contact link, on every page of the site, provide subject-sensitive help for complex tasks, ensure that the reader can avoid making errors, provide a progress chart where navigation moves have been made, optionally choose to provide chart navigations where processes are involved or provide options for contact or feedback. Navigation can be complex due to an overabundance of information. A Web site should always include a homepage, with paths such as a drop-down menu and language options. *Classified navigation* is your main source of information, and it is at the top of a Web page. It simply assists in directing the investor to the right page so if you click on 401(k)s , then you will be redirected to a 401(k) page.

Since the investment world has a lot to offer, it is likely any type of investment Web site would be considered the *"core"* of the system. This means there is a lot of information to sift through. This type of navigation is usually presented in the left-hand column of a homepage in alphabetical order however in an investment site; it may be presented in the middle or the right site. It really depends on the designer, but it is rare to see it on the right side. People tend to read from left to right. Other options include *drop-downs*, which are used as a space saving tool. These are not made to frustrate the Internet searcher, but should be use to classify a subject in a lower level of a class. This is known as a support tool for the entire site. Anytime "e-commerce" is mentioned, it means there is money involved but it includes extra things too. You are shopping, checking-out, buying stocks, viewing your account, or you just need help with something. Since we are all investors we will say you are buying a stock. E-commerce is actually one of the hottest developments of the Internet. Stocks for online-sales companies have also soared due to the Internet. In 1998, Amazon's sales increased an astonishing 966 percent.

The most important part of a Web site is its *homepage*. It supplies the reader with most contexts and as a road map to finding other things. If the home page is messed up, then the entire experience with the Web site will be a disaster. These sites do exist. The key highlights of each site are presented on the first page with a hypertext link. Hypertext is the links that can be clicked to redirect the reader elsewhere. *Global navigation* includes that of which everyone is included and catered to. ING Clarion's web site is a good example of this. The reader can go and choose the country in which a certain language is desired. The most used language is typically the default page.

In reviewing the **www.dowjones.com** Web site, the reader will notice that there are six main tabs to assist in being organized. Whatever it is the reader is looking for should be organized under these tabs, and while each page is reviewed, no matter what it is that is being viewed, the advanced search, contact us, language options, and search tool are always available at the top of every page.

Web site designers often have a unique artistic ability in which they seek to be different. With an investment Web site however, these designers often use the same skills as others where navigation seems easy, after all, that is the ultimate goal. To make a long story short, a good Web site will have the right content, quality content, comprehensive content, online community activities (perhaps an investment club), and update content. Nothing bugs me more, than to go to a Web site that has old information - especially with press releases where the latest was from three years ago. This is not a good business practice. Stock market exchange sites are a whole other story. They are updated daily. That is just the way the game is played.

SEARCH ENGINES

A good example for financial assistance is with Yahoo's financial search engine. Once you click on finance, you have tons of options: market summary for many countries, a search options by your stocks ticker symbol, news about the blues or stock ups and downs, as well as stories about the industry. Everything is available under direction. The investing tab helps whether you are looking at stocks, mutual funds, or whatever it may be; it is all there. The Web site also tells on what stocks are bullish and bearish, to date. Google is also quick in that once you retrieve the site, you just click on the more option and a finance options is made available. Instead of bulls and bears it lists losers and gainers and the organization seems much simpler, although it does not have as much to offer. This site represents the bare necessities, those that are needed the most plus the news. The quotes, which are probably the most searched for daily anyway, are displayed in both search engines.

INVESTMENT RESEARCH SITES:

www.briefing.com

EdgarOnline
www.edgar-online.com

Hoover's Online
www.hoovers.com

Hulbert Financial District
www.hulbertdigest.com

Investor Communications Business
www.icbinc.com

Market Guide
www.marketguide.com

Multex
www.multexinvestor.com

Public Register's Annual Reporter Service
www.prars.com

Quicken.com
www.quicken.com

Thomas Financial
www.thomsoninvest.com

Wall Street City

www.wallstreetcity.com

Zacks Investment Research

www.zacks.com

CASE STUDY: SHRAVAN GOLI

Senior Director of Yahoo Finance

http://finance.yahoo.com/ "We are the most comprehensive source for financial data and the most well recognized and trusted brand," said Shravan Goli, senior director of Yahoo! Finance.

The Web site offers more than enough information to investors of all sorts whether they are new investors or chief executive officers, not to mention brokerages. The site offers tools of all natures including mock portfolios in which investors can practice stock investments. The tool allows people to view all their stocks and holdings as if they were actually in existence. It gives a better feel of decisions made and capabilities of companies while learning the process. Through hypothetical information, decision-making skills can become stronger in addition to utilizing other tools such as news and other things available on the same site.

The stock quotes are the most sought after tool used on a daily basis, but the team is always ahead of the game with comprehensive information. Tech Ticker is the latest tool recently launched surrounding technology and video. Since technology is a very popular subject and trend, people follow it. The tool brings technological stock analyst opinions together that is not available elsewhere. Through video, professional analysts and columnists provide information. These columnists are from various sources including Business Week. The site offers up-to-date information through financial writers and bloggers. And there is interesting information available such as "new ways to invest." The site itself is free, but there are some things that cost such as research or analyst reports, which are an outside source.

CASE STUDY: SHRAVAN GOLI

An education center is available for first time investors including "investment 101" advice which covers all types of assets whether its stock investments, mutual fund information or retirement news; it is there. Exchanges include the U.S. and those all over the world. As always, the nice thing about the Web is that people from all over can access information. There is a lot of international traffic on this site. All in all, there are experts galore and experts are in the communities, including message board data. Regarding the message rooms, "People have different interpretations and supporting arguments and the experts provide a more focused analysis," said Goli. It seems Yahoo! Finance is another great Web site to be.

ELECTRONIC COMMUNICATION NETWORKS

It was decided by the SEC in 1998 that a computer system was need to help with the trading of financial things aside from the stock exchanges, particularly for stocks and currencies. The phenomenon brings competition among trading firms. It also lowers transaction costs. The ECN allows investors to trade outside of business hours while giving them access the all-pertinent information. Investors must be a subscriber to the network and at that point, he/she can enter orders into the network in which it will request matches. If a match does not take place, then other subscribers are able to view those preferences with an option to negotiate.

Previously mentioned, there is no spread between the matching of the buyers and sellers of the network. A quarter here and there will add up quickly for those who are regulars. For the private investors, ECNs may not be that beneficial due to the illiquidity, meaning it is not good for a heavy cash flow.

An investor could consider an investment club a tool. Sometimes we get by with a little help from our friends. There are investment clubs where there at least two investors put together in making the right investment choices. Members of investment clubs meet regularly to discuss investment opportunities and the stock market in general. A good club size would be about 15 people, as meetings are usually conducted in homes or in any accommodating location. Legally, a maximum is 20 members. Clubs members usually commit a specific amount of time on a monthly basis. Among these clubs, there is a president, vice president, financial treasurer, and secretary. Often times there are education officers. I guess the fun thing about these clubs is that they are personable; you can make friends with the same interest levels as you all have something in common, and you can call your club whatever you want. These groups are nice because although it seems fun, the members also get down to business as the one with the financial responsibilities communicates regularly with a brokerage in which stock is bought and sold. The treasurer is also responsible for financial records, which present everyone's assets and status. If there is an educational officer, then quite often these clubs will take trips where there are speakers on the subject, or presentations are held, further educating the members. The secretary keeps track of minutes, meetings, and any other office activities that are relevant for the club. Members are all able to vote and decide on any group decision by a majority vote. The president plans meeting and activities while the vice president assists and does the same. Investment clubs are typically organized as partnerships. Investment clubs do not have to register with the SEC, as it is a little more informal; however it is up

to the members to decide on registering, as some s[e]
laws can apply. It is required that investment clubs register
under the SEC if it would be considered an "investment
company," and due to the Investment Company Act of
1940 the club would need to register based on a few things.
This includes on any basis that the club is investing in
securities, the club has membership interests that are
security assets, and that the club is "not able to rely on the
exclusion from the definition of the investment company."
Another law that needs to be taken into consideration is
the Securities Act of 1933. With this, on any condition that
there is an investment contract where profit is expected
from the investors, there is a membership interest. And
as long as there is a membership interest, then it is up
to the members to decide if there are securities. This is to
determine on whether or not every member of the club is
in tune with what investments to allocate to. If everyone
is not on the same page, this means securities are being
issued. Depending on the situation, some securities are
exempt under the law.

A good learning experience for an investor is to become
a member of the National Association of Investors
Corporation (NAIC). Its Web site is at **www.better-
investing.org**. Its primary focus is the investment club
world while educating the investor as well as those in
clubs. By joining an investment club, the investor can
learn market fundamentals. Usually those that are in
investment clubs have a lot of money to invest. On the
other hand, with pooling everyone's money within the
club, investors get opportunities to invest wisely in ways
they might not otherwise be able to do. The clubs are not

meant for people who have a "get rich quick" mind frame. Members do contribute a reasonable monthly description and are always entitled to pull out of the club selling that individuals share at the current price.

Motley Fool is an example of an investment club that is well known (**www.fool.com**). Within the Web site, there are discussion boards, quotes, updated information on the stock indexes, news topics, stock advisor's services, and more. The site offers a lot of educational opportunities anywhere from how to value stocks to doing taxes. The company began in 1993 with every intention of educating investors. Today, the company has over 200 employers in both the United States and the UK. These employees offer investment advice and financial information.

CASE STUDY: CHRIS HILL

Director of Media and Communications

www.fool.com

Chill@fool.com

2000 Duke St., Floor 4

Alexandria, VA 22314

Fax: 703.254.1999

Discussion boards among Motley Fool involve investment clubs. There are thousands of discussion boards that focus on individuals stocks. The Web site is unique as those investors cannot only go to the Web site for advice, but people can also join other clubs such a movies or television. One of the most popular boards regards "quitting smoking." The company itself is not an investment club alone but a service in which financial advice is offered. Within the past year, Motley launched a service called CAPS beta.

CASE STUDY: CHRIS HILL

This is a recognized rating system where over 70,000 investors dicuss analysis and communication. The Web site offers endless information such as stocksand rate them on a five-star scale. And within all the investors' involved, there is a percentage rating system that rates those individuals on the performance of their actual choices. Information is also combines from Wall Street sources making decision even better. Chris Hill of Motley Fool, says he is in the 32 percentile range which means 68 percent or more is doing better than he. But that does not stop him from being a member. Hill said the best advice is to "go with what you know," regarding stock brands. By this, brands such as Coca-Cola and Johnson & Johnson, which have been around for years versus something low-key that has never been heard of.

Although another advantage that Motley Fool offers is information on those stocks that fly under the radar with some of the major exchanges. There are many stocks out there that are ignored because they are not a large company. There are a lot of small-cap and midcap companies that are not covered on those indexes. People visit Motley mainly for investment ideas in addition to retirement planning tips or education. Investment tools are readily available. "People use CAPS beta as a great second opinion regardless of if they have a broker or not," Hill said. The top ten and low ten are also covered with Wall Street business while up-to-date information is consistently covered with individual reporters within Motley Fool plus those feeds that are available from the Associated Press. A typical news story states the facts of any given situation while Motley Fool news stories offer analysis and commentaries. People like this when a "what does this mean" question pops up. While there are many discussion boards out there where scamming can take place or negativity, Motley Fool has fulltime moderators on all boards. This way there is no profanity or hyping of stocks. Members are also allowed to notify when there is something he/she feels is not appropriate. There are no discussion boards for penny stocks. The boards have a subscription service anywhere from $99 to $500. Newsletter received among the members can be both online and via direct mail and pdfs can even be printed if an investor choices to print it before receiving a direct mail copy. Investment clubs tend to meet once a month. They share

CASE STUDY: CHRIS HILL
articles as a discussion point making everyone's time valuable. "Think about what you know and already understand with your investments and take your time in doing so," said Hill.

CAPS EXAMPLES	
INVESTMENT STRATEGIES	INDUSTRY DISCUSSIONS
FOOLISH 401(K)S	FINANCIAL PRODUCTS AND SERVICES
RETIRED FOOLS	DISCOUNT BROKERS
CANSLIM INVESTING	DRIP INVESTING
THE BASICS	PERSONAL FINANCES
LIVING BELOW YOUR MEAN	INVESTMENT ANALYSIS CLUBS
LEARNING TO INVEST	

YAHOO AND SILICON INVESTOR

Another popular site includes Yahoo Finance (finance. yahoo.com). In comparison to Motley Fool, the Web site does not disclose information about the visiting readers, but Motley has over a million visitors to its site on a monthly basis. Yahoo remains one of the most popular places on the net, finance or not, and message boards, chat rooms, and postings continue to take place among the investor groups. Motley keeps a sharp eye on what goes in the message boardroom, but the Yahoo Finance department has been criticized about some of the messages that have been posted that should be allowed. That does not mean the information is not accurate or beneficial. Yahoo is free while another company, Silicon Investor (**www. siliconinvestor.com**), charges $60 a year for its services.

The Web site is another chat site whereas message boards are available and chosen topics of investor discussions take place.

FINANCE CALCULATORS

ADR.com
www.adr.com

Armchair Millionaire
www.armchairmillionaire.com

Financenter
www.financenter.com

Financial Engines
www.financialengines.com

Gomez Advisors
www.gomezadvisors.com

InvestorGuide
www.investorguide.com

Media General Financial Services
www.mgfs.com

Microsoft Money Central
Moneycentral.msn.com

Network Solutions
www.netwroksolutions.com

SmartMoney.com
www.smartmoney.com

Virtual University of Investing
www.virtual-u.com

With investment clubs, they can often cater to people who have additional interests such as saving the environment.

(1) **www.better-investing.org/**

A non-profit organization, this site, caters to volunteer-based investors while offering classes and tools while assisting in investment decisions.

(2) **www.myiclub.com/**

This Web site offers software that can assist with investment club stock portfolios as well as individual investors. "Over 100,000 investors use ICLUBcentral's software, a larger installed base than any other investing software company. In addition, 15,000 investment clubs (80 percent of the market) use ICLUBcentral's software for portfolio management and tax preparation."

(3) **www.investmentclubhelp.com/**

If you want to start your own investment club, this site tells you how. This site helps the investor find other club members while assisting with business models. The site further elaborates on investment clubs in general with recommended software.

(4) **www.reiclub.com/**

This Web site has all kinds of stuff. It is all about the real estate though.

This club recommends specific books to expand knowledge, offers discussion forums, in addition to investment articles. Newsgroup forums include opportunities for beginners, asset protection, and more.

CASE STUDY: KARIN HOUSLEY

Founder

http://www.chickslayingnesteggs.com/

Lakeland, Minnesota

"My parents didn't talk about money," said Karin Housley, founder of the investment group Chicks Laying Nest Eggs. Housley said this caused a light to come on for her and she taught her kids about the stock market while making it fun for them. With a couple of teenagers, buying stock in Gap or Abercrombie can be fun. This sparks an interest in kids early on. Even one of the two youngest keeps a sharp eye on what is happening with the Disney stock because it is fun and educational at the same time. A Minnesota mom, Housley's second daughter (at a young age) has served on a school stock market team in which her team won. It pays off to teach the children young. Four kids ranging from 10 to 21-years-of-age all have portfolios. Housley feels parents should teach the kids, and even if they do not know at the age of 40, it is OK. There is nothing wrong with baby steps The club itself has been in existence since 1998 and it has been successful. Chick Housley wanted to get together with girlfriends. An online club allow for all the chicks near or far to communicate on a monthly basis. The chicks are scattered all over including states of Georgia, Florida, Maine, Illinois, Arizona, and even Canada. These chicks have made it fun while making

CASE STUDY: KARIN HOUSLEY

money though traveling to shows, sharing books, and selling chick pajamas. Occasionally, the team meets in one location to make sure all the eggs are covered. Upon the initial meeting, the team had read a few investment books and with a vote, great minds were combined and out came an investment strategy. The team used tools with Motley Fool and message boards from America Online.

Determined to not become overwhelmed by the terminology of the market the chicks just decided to write a book in a successful attempt forcing all of them to learn as much as they could. The focus of the book was "how to start an investment club." Confused, as most first-time investors are, the combination of ten minds made it happen for this group. The investment strategy for the girls' is such that once a month, everyone allocates $50 to a voted upon investment. The chicks are your everyday people with busy lives, children, and husbands to take care of and they are not the type to spend a lot of time doing PE ratios or timing the market on an exact time to buy or sell. They are all in for the long run with a long-term investment. The women in the group really delve into the history of the companies they choose, as well as management moves and/or changes. Since the chicks are busy, the stock in question is that which will sit and grow. Aside from investments, when the chicks have time they do community service while working with Habitat for Humanity, for example, or in a breast cancer event. Nine chicks is enough for these girls, but they are available to and in January I 2008, seminars are available online that will assist with those who are interested in starting their own investment club. In other matters allgeneraquestions are available too such as "learn what the stock market is and why it is the best place to put your money."

"It's not as overwhelming as I thought n the beginning and having other friends to bounce what I though were stupid question, I didn't feel intimidated," Housley said. Great advice from Housley "Start with people you know and trust already, otherwise clubs don't gel and then there are conflicting views. These women that I knew at some point in my life and brought them all together."

The chicks meet in Omaha, Nebraska with new incentives.

THE CHICKS' 12 STEPS TO PICKING A STOCK

STEP 1 | BUY WHAT YOU KNOW

How well do you know it, how often do you use it and how much do you like it?

STEP 2 | K.I.S.S.

Keep it simple sister. Can you easily explain the products industry to your cute little niece? Can you draw it with a crayon?

STEP 3 | INDUSTRY

Who are its competitors? Is the industry growing faster than other industries? Do you understand it?

STEP 4 | LEADER IN ITS FIELD

Is the company top dog in its industry? Is it the leader of the pack?

(Sing it with me: leader of the pack... vroooom, vroooom)

STEP 5 | REPEAT PROFITABILITY

Is this a company that has an opportunity to make a profit from its customers time after time? Will consumers use it again and again or over and over? (Be honest, how many cola beverages do you drink?)

STEP 6 | GROSS MARGINS

Are gross margins at least 50%?

STEP 7 | NET MARGINS

Are net margins at least 8%?

STEP 8 | CASH TO LONG TERM DEBT

Does the company have more cash than long term debt?

STEP 9 | FLOW RATIO

Is the company's flow ratio better than 1.5?

STEP 10 | INCREASING GROWTH

STEP 11 | STRONG MANAGEMENT AND HISTORY

Who are the people running the company? What have

they done? Do you like what they stand for? What is the company's history?

STEP 12 | ON SALE

Is its stock price lower than its 52-week average?

IT IS THE SOCIAL THING TO DO

The interview with the Chicks Laying Nest Eggs club proves that investing can be a fun and social event as well. More and more people are becoming interest in the subject matter. At times people have hard times with the finances leaving the only solution to money expansion. There are colleges, schools and classes available that offer investment education. You just have to find them because not all of them are up to par. There are games on the Internet as well where you can "practice" or incorporate the paper money theory. By having an investment club, risks are spread and the basics can be explained more thoroughly. All profits are shared and split among the members of the clubs. Since people are a little uneasy about investing at first, bringing up other matters, interests and likes can put minds at ease. In addition, the investing helps the economy as investors are supporting businesses.

MESSAGE BOARD WEB SITES:

Deja.com

mIRC.com

Motley Fool
www.fool.com

Raging Bull
www.ragingbull.com

Silicon Investor
www.siliconinvestor.com

Yahoo! Finance
Finance.yahoo.com

Bank One
www.bankone.com

Countrywide Credit Industries
www.countrywide.com

E-loan
www.eloan.com

HomeAdvisor
www.homeadvisor.com

HSH Associates
www.hsh.com

Keystroke.com
www.keystroke.com

LendingTree
www.lendingtree.com

Priceline
www.priceline.com

Quicken
www.quickenloans.quicken.com

iQualify.com
www.iqualify.com

RealEstate.com
www.realestate.com

Rock Loans
www.rockloans.com

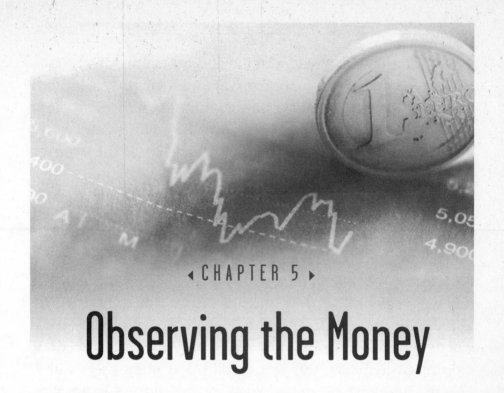

CHAPTER 5

Observing the Money

Sometimes it is hard for a first time investor to have faith in an IRA broker to manage their money. You will never know if he or she is good until something goes wrong. An example of this would be when the dot.com bubble happened in the mid-1990s to 2001 and many stocks plummeted to an all-time low. Thanks to the Internet, the not-so-interesting stocks lost many investors as they were pulling out and putting into these new dot-com Internet business stocks. I am certain there were some who had brokers at that time who just were not quick enough in making the trade or selling things. There were stocks that were over-inflated, but it took a while for things to go from well over $100 to $5 per share. While the investor should have paid more attention, a good advisor would have too. The most common misunderstanding among first time investors is "what makes the market take a big dive?" This concept is hard to grasp. You are just an investor with plans for the future, not a financial major. Obviously, it is due to the economy, but there are the "who knows why" instances in which nobody knows, or at least the average investor does not know.

If Dow Jones takes a big tumble, it does not always affect your holdings, it may or it may not. If you have a large mutual fund where the stocks are diversified enough, these factors may not even affect your portfolio. The typical direct investor looks at his/her mutual funds and compares the amount of money that they are worth to what they were worth the month prior. It is really only necessary to do it on a monthly basis, but you can do it as often as you like. Using *Vanguard, T. Rowe Price,* or *Fidelity* as examples, these advisors will reinvest your dividends as a standard procedure on a quarterly basis. In researching the Web sites of these companies, and looking at the different offerings in mutual funds, the first time investor will look at those that seem to be performing the best. Charts usually show progress over a long-term period showing what percentage that company is increasing share value by specific time periods. This gives an idea as to past performance. In addition, they also show what mutual funds seem safer. The more aggressive the fund, the higher the risk, but these have the nicest returns. Those funds that invest in foreign countries are really risky because if the government there is overthrown or a war breaks out in that country, your mutual fund could drop considerably. These are the kinds of chances the investor takes. In setting buy and sell prices, consider those companies with price-earning ratios that are no higher than the annual rate of earnings.

An example would be if the earnings are $5 per share and it grows by 10 percent in a year, the investor should not purchase it for more than $50. If an investor owns this stock and it exceeds this amount then it might be the time to sell for a profit. If a stock looks like it is starting to decrease, the investor should set a loss level where there is an alert system, warning a selling point in which case there could be a slight loss. One alternative is to use a broker who would provide an alert service.

Common investing mistakes are ignoring investments until there is a market rally, and buying when the price is just too high. Selling when the market is going down and selling prematurely is another mistake as the market ends up going back up. Do not become obsessed with a stock in thoughts that it will payoff. It is not good to stick with this stock when it is bad. Be weary about stories about some who got rich quickly with a certain stock. This is meant for the investor to follow other footsteps that may actually lead nowhere.

SOFTWARE OPPORTUNITIES VERSUS BROKERS

Often times, people use monitor-investing software which assists in keeping up with the portfolio whether or not a broker exists. It is an investment tool that does record keeping, alerts, e-mail notifications, news alerts, and management options. Brokers use these programs, too. A huge advantage to these programs, for those that are weak in the tax area, is such that your programs can keep you organized for when the tax season does arrive. The National Association of Investors Corporation makes it easy for use in that it too offers investment programs, keeping tabs on industries and companies sifting the bad and the good. While TurboTax has been a good friend of mine for the last few years, some other personal finance program examples include MS Money, Quicken, and Moneydance. These help you with your tax issues also.

This software can be purchased individually but it often comes with a new computer. A few nice things, these programs allow the investor to become willfully organized in all checking accounts, while managing all investments and paying bills on the Internet. The investor can download everything from their bank, including current deposits and written checks. These systems assist in retirement planning decisions, and portfolio investments with exquisite detail. With any type of investment, you are covered. The good thing about having these programs is that they are at your convenience. These software programs make it easier to get background information on brokerages and banks.

Looking into the Microsoft Money program, for example, other benefits include up-to-date information on Wall Street's watch where there is a Market Report: Stock Ticker. The market news is available through stock tickers, story stocks, and more, while market statistic options, including lists and trends, currency tools, and calendars, are made handy too. News by topic is made available on specific companies and stocks themselves while keeping up with the economy in general. With IPOs, you can view what is new and upcoming while reading the filings performances and highlights of the phenomena. Market upgrade and downgrade information helps in making a choice on whether to sell or stay with a stock. And then there is an

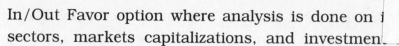

In/Out Favor option where analysis is done on i
sectors, markets capitalizations, and investmen.
This should be in tune with the current market trends
of stock performances. All in all, the system is extremely
convenient in a lot of ways. On the primary screen, the
first thing that comes up is the Dow Jones, NASDAQ, and
S&P indexes, your tools, your portfolio, and the top news
stories. What more could you ask? The report tab of the
software is especially nice for taxing purposes; you can keep
us with the capital gains and anything else tax-related.
You can monitor your investment portfolio by asset type,
its performance as well as summary, and your spending
habits can be obtained as well, making it easier to work
with yourself and your annual budget.

PORTFOLIO OBSERVATION PROGRAMS

It seems like no one should complain about much
of anything any more; our culture is presented with
alternatives to everything. There are many options for
everything since everyone has their own tastes, and
portfolio investment software is one of those things. These
are for the independents who can do without (or with) a
broker. This software offers prepackaged options in which
the investor can purchase an already-prepared portfolio
involving securities. The other advantage to these programs
is that they are cheaper than a brokerage fee. An investor
automatically gains access to tons of stocks and will have
full knowledge of exactly what investment is involved.
Sometimes with mutual funds or brokers, the investor
may not know what is going on half of the time. They are
just walking down the road whistling and looking up at the

clouds. As an owner of these programs, the investor still has choices in what the desired requirements are. The new investor could also refer to it as another learning system as a few stocks may be chosen, but maybe it is not enough for diversifying the portfolio. This software will do that.

Note: See **www.foliofn.com.**

STOCK	# SHARES	ORIGINAL COST	WORTH TODAY	% CHANGE
APOLLO GROUP (APOL)	27	$1,798.47	$1,572.21	-12.59%
BIOMET (BMET)	105	$3,352.30	$4,778.55	42.55%
BERKSHIRE B (BRK.B)	8	$20,646.89	$28,796.00	39.47%
BUFFALO WILD WINGS INC (BWLD)	22	$958.63	$789.58	-17.63%
CSX CORP (CSX)	50	$1,607.27	$2,397.50	49.17%
DELL INC (DELL)	70	$2,018.99	$1,943.20	-3.75%
DREW INDS INC (DW)	75	$1,945.450	$2,844.00	46.19%
EBAY INC (EBAY)	100	$4,101.95	$3,278.00	-20.09%
ISHARES FTSE/ XINHUA CHINA (FXI)	44	$5,457.22	$6,036.80	10.62%
HOME DEPOT INC (HD)	50	$1,918.95	$1,888.50	-1.59%

STOCK	# SHARES	ORIGINAL COST	WORTH TODAY	% CHANGE
LULUEMON ATHLETICA INC (LULU)	85	$2,571.89	$2,641.80	2.72%
MEDTRONIC INC (MDT)	76	$3,440.92	$3,983.92	15.78%
SELECT COMFORT CORP (SCSS)	62	$1,284.09	$1,039.74	-19.03%
VOLCOM INC (VLCM)	64	$1,609.99	$2,426.24	50.70%
WALGREEN CO (WAG)	101	$3,994.89	$4,517.73	13.09%
WHOLE FOODS MKT INC (WFMI)	45	$2,034.99	$1,778.40	-12.61%
WEBZEN INC (WZEN)	214	$1,101.39	$1,110.66	0.84%
EXXON MOBILE CORP (XOM)	24	$1,565.67	$2,403.46	20.31%

CASE STUDY: ARTICLE

Written by Michelle Hooper

(Crittenden Publishing Inc.)

Nov. 2007

This article shows a deep analysis of investment portfolios and returns of state pension systems, in a timely manner. A core portfolio represents a blend of stock. Since pensions represent several individuals, it is important that the appointed advisors stay on top of the game because there are thousands of people involved here.

AN INSIDE LOOK INTO THE WORK OF OUR PENSION SYSTEMS

Pension funds show the greatest interest in core, non-core and global opportunities in the upcoming year as returns are expected to be positive. A recent retirement systems survey showed a median return of 2.3 percent for first-quarter returns. Some pension funds begin to make room for commercial real estate in their portfolios whether it is in commercial-backed mortgages or direct real estate investments. The Ohio State Teachers' Retirement System and Illinois Municipal Retirement Fund had a rocky start in real estate stock since it plummeted earlier this year, but because the Fed made some well-needed changes, this saved a few portfolios from losses. Meanwhile, returns are still coming in for fiscal year third quarters and for the most part, they are looking good.

The Hawaii Employees' Retirement System has done exceptionally well for its first quarter, which began in July. The pension system had a 3.3-percent gain, exceeding its benchmark of 2.9 percent, bringing its total portfolio assets to $11.7B. The pension had a good fiscal year for 2007 with double-digit returns, which has turned into a trend the past four years. The domestic and fixed-income class of the portfolio is what really pushed the returns higher for the third quarter. In the domestic equity department, all 13 managers surpassed their benchmarks in addition to boosts from 12 of 13 U.S. equity managers over-performing from the trailing 12 months. The first quarter benchmark was 2.9 percent. Hawaii ERS boosted its assets to $11.7B, up from 2007 fiscal year of $11.6B.

The Alaska Permanent Fund also gained positively for its first quarter period ending Sept. 30. The portfolio now possesses $38.9B in assets, with the last month being the exception to the rule when the fund saw a 3.2 percent return. Like Hawaii, this pension really performed well in the fixed-income (stock) sector as the U.S. portfolio returned a 2.8 percent and the non-U.S. portfolio returned 5.1 percent. The real estate portfolio saw a gain of 1.7 percent. The subprime mortgage market really took its toll on the pension system in July when the stock markets began crashing; thankfully, the Federal Reserve Board lowered primary credit rates and federal funds causing the stocks to roar upward again. The pension funds stocks also had positive returns of 1.8 percent domestic and 2.2 percent global.

The Teacher Retirement System of Texas finished its 2007 fiscal year at the end of August with a total portfolio return of 14.4 percent beating the objectives of 8 percent and bringing its portfolio to $111.1B. Investment income totals $14.3B with an overall gain of $52M during its five-year presence. While many pensions have been making long-term objectives for long-term risk tolerances, the biggest change this pension fund made, set until 2011, is the addition of a 3-percent allocation to real estate equity funds or joint venture investment goals. A focus on alternative investments will take place accounting for 8.5 percent of the total fund. Changes are made for portfolio diversification, meant to gain higher returns. In August 2005, the entire portfolio was $93.7B. At that point, returns were consistent and above average for nine out of ten years.

ALLOCATIONS FLOW IN

Arizona State Teachers' Retirement System has allocated $150M to Blackstone Real Estate Partners VI L.P., Tishman Speyer Real Estate Ventures VII, L.P. and CIM Fund III, LLC for its non-core portfolio since June 30. The only investment strategy the pension has changed is its $140M U.S. public securities portfolio, when it changed advisors. Aside from the pension funds direct investing habits, it tends to carry more weight in the office sector, which represents over half of the real estate portfolio, shadowing all of its real estate investment moves. Geographic diversification will include all regional areas evenly.

Pennsylvania State Employees Retirement System makes more allocations on the heels of its 22 percent fiscal year return. The first half of this year investment returns showed an 11.4 percent with 6 percent of that in the second quarter alone. The latest allocations include $30M to Fillmore's West Fun, L.P., $100M to New York Life Capital Partners IV, L.P. and an estimated $70M to Nordic Capital Fund VII. Fillmore is the only real estate fund. Pramerica Real Estate Partners have recently launched a Mexico fund in which Pennsylvania SERS has shown an interest but has not yet made any investments.

A direct investor in industrial real estate properties, the Illinois Municipal Retirement Fund has been doing well with recent allocations of $100M to Morgan Stanley's Prime Property Fund and another $100M to BlackRock's Granite Fund for its core real estate portfolio. For the fiscal year 2006, which ended Dec.31, returns for the entire portfolio were at 13.9 percent with a decent real estate return of 24.9 percent. At this time, fourth quarter, year-to-date returns for the third quarter rolled in at 8.9 percent while real estate showed 9.4 percent. The pension fund contributes its success to a focus on industrial properties, core real estate and opportunistic senior housing. These sectors have brought the most significant returns, bringing confidence for the New Year with no plans for strategy changes. The entire portfolio represents $24.5B of assets (Phew, the end.).

SCREENING

Stock screening is somewhat neat. It allows you to do the research that matches your investment needs in a short amount of time. If you have a lot to look up, a stock screener allows the investor to look up many things all at once. These programs scan thousands of stocks and limit them to as few as 20 to meet the investors' qualifications. Of course, there are subscription packages involved with these. After clarification on the stock that meets the investor's intentions, the programs can find things by industry, market capitalizations, dividends, and more. As always, the more expensive the program, the more benefits, but that is not to say less expensive programs cannot work just as well. One man's junk could be another man's gold. Tighter qualifications in these programs would minimize the risk of having too much information. These screeners finger through those opportunities throughout the entire major exchanges. In reviewing MSN money, a few examples, the investor can go as far as entering a dividend yield expectation, debt/equity ratio, and net profit margin. This should also include financial statistics about a company and filtered variables.**www.msnmoney.com**

Unfortunately, stock screeners are not the most reliable source. And just because the investor is screening information does not mean everything will turn out wonderfully. A good screener should meet the investor's objectives. Some things are not measured, including information on interest rates, inflation rates, lawsuits, or any other random thing that may take deeper research. It is another decision where the options need to be weighed. Since it is called a "screening" process the search filters out all the unfit candidates. To make a long story short, this is not needed if you have a broker. That does not mean it should not be looked into. Financial ratios are a big part of the screening routine. They are the biggest comparison among companies. Within this analysis, stock performances are observed, sales, profitability, value ratios, growth rates, and share data are reviewed. That is a lot of work to be done in such a short amount of time. Should anything change among the retrieved stocks to the investors benefit, this information becomes available as well with an explanation as to why. Among other things, this is just another option to consider.

Some of the important ratios in stock screening are earnings growth, which is the percentage of change between the earnings for either the last year or the previous quarter and the current earnings. This includes recent earning surprises, which is actual earnings or predicted earning and the difference. Price to earnings ratio is also part of the mix, which is when the stocks current price divided by earnings per share. With dividends, actual cash is paid to the stockholder while market capitalization represents the current price of the stock times the number of outstanding shares. Other criteria than can be used in stock screening consist of beta; this is how much the price of the stock changes in relation to the overall stock market. It shows how volatile the stock is. Beta can be calculated by comparing the historical price movements with general index movements. The beta of 1.0 is exactly the same risk as the general market. If the market goes up 5 percent, then this beta of 1.0 will be expected to also rise 5 percent. The same would hold true for the market falling. A beta of 2.0 would cause a stock to rise 6 percent if the market was to increase by 3 percent and the same applies if the market declines.

The book value of a stock company is also taken into consideration with screening, as it is the company's original costs less its cumulated depreciation. Subtracting from a shareholder's equity and the liquidation value of owed preferred dividends and preferred stock, and then dividing that result by the number of outstanding common shares calculate a book value per share. There are Web sites available that sift through the bond selections as well. These options are free but do not be surprised if there is a sales pitch somewhere along the way. With mutual fund screening, an investor can still quickly go through thousands of funds in just seconds. Lists are provided with the requested specifics, just as you would in screening stocks, although there are fewer choices. The main and most important searched variables include investment strategies, costs, assets, performance returns, and ratings.

STOCK AND MUTUAL FUND SCREENER WEB SITES

www.bondvillage.com

www.bonds.yahoo.com

www.cbsmarketwatch.com

www.forbes.com

www.mfea.com

www.money.com

www.moneycentral.msn.com

www.morningstar.com

www.quicken.com

www.screen.yahoo.com

www.smartmaoney.com

www.zacks.com

OTHER OBSERVATIONS

With a cash flow to share price analysis ratio, it is when the net income of a company plus depreciation is divided by an outstanding number of shares. Cash flow may be considered a company's most important financial statistic as it represent status and good targets for takeovers, where other corporations can come in and take over the company.

Meanwhile, to find the current ratio of a company, an investor can divide the current assets by current liabilities. A company's balance sheet will provide this information. If the ratio were 1.00 or more, the company can pay its current obligations and not use future earnings. And a debt-to-equity ratio is determined by dividing long-term debt by equity total. Equity itself is the ownership interest in a company where preferred stockholders and creditors have been paid. A better financial stability is shown through a low debt-to-equity ratio.

Shares outstanding are the total number of shares of a company stock. This is done by taking the issued shares from a balance sheet and subtracting treasury stock (stock issued but held by the company). Once this is done you have the outstanding shares.

PORTFOLIO MANAGER SOFTWARE

The same goes with portfolio manager software where there are more than enough features and great investment tracking options.

WEB SITES

www.quicken.com

www.moneydance.com

www.microsoft.com

More mutual fund stocks are purchased with dividends, and it is your job to make the decision on whether the advisor is making money for you. If not, it may be time to look elsewhere and sell that investment. If, for example, your mutual fund is invested in mostly foreign countries or mining, you can make a lot with mining short-term or long-term, but it is risky with high volatility. Hopefully, a mutual fund will continue to keep going up in value because by reinvesting the dividends you get more shares, and if those go up in value and you sell, you make more money.

In an IRA observation, these have mutual funds in which a statement is received once a month, updating on anything that drops in value. As there is a set amount of money taken out each month, if the money market fund is getting low then you should speak with your financial advisor about selling something to counteract not having enough money to withdraw for your monthly income. This is typical of retired people. Since IRAs pay with a much smaller percentage, these mutual funds are more stable and reliable. You can have an IRA that invests in anything, but you need an income-type mutual fund if you want a monthly income. Scottrade will allow options in penny stocks. These should be analyzed on a daily basis in comparison to a watch list, which provides a ticker symbol and how many shares you own and what they are worth each day, which you can only have if you have your own account. Sometimes a market limit order is necessary daily with these penny stocks if they are believed to go up. So, if you are stock selling for 15 cents a share, and you want to make money by selling at 17 cents a share, then you could place this limit order for the day or until you cancel it. This pot should be for money you can afford to loose, though it can be a good opportunity to make a very nice profit in a short amount of time. Penny stocks are also known for mining ventures.

British Columbia, Salt Lake City, and Utah are popular to those mining ventures.

RATES OF RETURNS

In reviewing a brokerage or stocks and the returns that are offered, this plays a big role in the decisions of an investment. While research is really what the investor needs to do, if the charts show negative amortization this is already a big turnoff. Often times, an investor will go with the one that has the highest numbers. For some, it is a natural instinct to be greedy, although it is not really a good thing. The internal rate of return (IRR) measures your returns over a period of time, which is expressed as an annual percentage rate. This can also be called the discount rate. The net present value of your investment equals the cost of the investment providing the interest rate. A financial planner may only use this formula to help in the decision to invest in something. It is a pre-determination of a company's cash flow. Let us say you are looking at Vanguard's Web site and you click on the mutual fund and ETFs link to compare some things, you pull funds up by asset class. At this point you can pull up money market funds, bonds, and securities and compare the year-to-date returns. From this you can see that the highest are the best. A portfolio statement will show you the percentage of assets on whatever time frame you are on.

POINTS

In observing your bond, future, stock, or even real estate

investments, points represent or may be referred to as face values, price changes, or interest rate changes. It is another way to make observations. With a bond, if there is a price changed it is explained as having increased or decreased by so many points. Therefore if a face value of a bond is $3000 and it increases in price by 2 percent, then your points have increased by 2 percent. With a futures contract, a contractual agreement made on the floor of a futures commodity in a buying or selling deal, point changes may be made in decimal form, meaning the price of a contract could change in increments of one point just as though it were in the dollar system. So if there is a contract that decreases by 30 points, then that is 30 cents. Regarding stocks, 5 points is $5. No percentages here, just dollars.

PRICE EARNINGS RATIOS

Investors use a price-earning ratio to determine whether a stock is worth their time. Expensive or cheap is the big question, and where does the company's earning power fit in. To determine the P/E ratio, you divide the latest closing stock price by the latest 12 months' earnings per share. It is the market value per share divided by earnings per share. If your shares are $30 and your earnings are $2 per share, the P/E ration would be 15.00.

A low P/E multiple would mean that a company has low growth prospects and a high P/E multiple. These ratios are compared to other companies. Those companies that seem to have higher ratios than similar companies do tend to have more money. It may also be an indication that higher returns are expected. This is not always wonderful news, as it also means there is a potentially higher risk in that particular company. A stock of this nature could lose its juice very quickly. If there is a low P/E ratio in a company, it means the stock price has fallen and does not really coincide with that company's profits, causing it to be disproportionate.

RETURN ON EQUITY AND ASSETS

This is another great tool in determining whether a company is performing that shareholders can calculate by dividing the latest 12 months' net income by the common-stock equity pertaining to the most recent quarter. It is the net income divided by the average stockholders equity. A company is doing well and using your money well if the return on equity is high and is continuing to rise. It all depends on what is going on within a particular company, a lucky day or month perhaps leading to a nice stock investment. With new products, a company may exceed the competition because the newer and the freshest is always more attractive. Yes, this applies to stock investments. If this equity starts falling, so will the stock price. A Return on Asset is when a company divides the last 12 months' net income by assets recorded within the most recent quarter. Simply put, it is the net income divided by total assets. This includes both the debt and equity of the company. If an ROA number is high, it means more is being earned altogether. It is all about how a company turns the assets into a profit for the shareholder.

SPREADS

A spread amongst stocks will vary, as heavily traded stocks tend to have smaller spreads, while thinly traded stocks typically have larger spreads. It is virtually the difference between the asking price and the bidding price in which the market maker (broker) is willing to buy. These brokers are specialist, representing an institution where stocks are bought and sold on temporary terms because they are quickly sold to make a profit. It also depends on the amount of shares being traded. Logically, investors tend to go for the stocks that seem the most popular, bidding more with intentions to quickly turn around and sell at an even higher price. The same goes if the stock seems idle, less attention will be focused. The NYSE never matches orders for the same price with a buy order, but will buy for more than the seller has asked. The broker receives the difference in these prices in exchange for providing a market for the security. In any case, an investor can reduce the amount lost to spreads by using limit orders. With an ECN, you can avoid the brokers that collect profit on these spreads. In contrast, a broker would be happy to provide an investor a market for a security in which the broker will receive that price between an ask and a bid. There are different kinds of spreads. A dealer spread is when the broker quotes for either the bid or the offer. This is the difference between the buying and selling. Meanwhile, an inside spread is the quote made by all the market makers for the highest bid and for the lowest offer. Third, actual spreads paid are actual trade prices measured against the inside quotes when the trade is made.

COMPOUNDS

Compounding is a significant part of investing, as it is what makes you have excellent investment returns. Since dividends and interest is earned with your stocks, compounding is taking place. If you save $50 a week and put it in a fund in which there was an average 12 percent return, at the end of 40 years you would have a lot of money. It is when you are earning or paying more interest on reinvested interests. If you start out with $1,000 and it is compounded yearly at 6 percent interest, at the end of the first year the investor would add $60 to the initial investment. The following year, the 6 percent interest would be paid on $1,060. From this point on, the investor will add the interest to the preceding year where interest gets paid on that amount. That said, the investment will increase for a long time until the investor redeems the stock. The more often that your investment is compounded, the more money you will make. A wise investor will look for an investment where compounding is done on a weekly basis rather than yearly. Yearly is still a good option, but those investments with weekly compounding will bring in more dough in the long run. An example of this comparison is $1,000 at 5 percent simple interest for one year would yield $1,050. Compounding weekly, would net an extra $1.27. After a 15-year period, this simple interest would net $2,078.90 and a weekly compound would be $2,116. 24.

INFLATION

Inflation is when the dollar bill gets bloated. Any kind of inflationary news will usually cause a drop in the stock markets, which would be a good time to buy because stock prices decrease. You should keep in mind that this affects the returns on an investment. Therefore, if an investment return is 14 percent and inflation set by the Consumer Price Index (CPI) is around 3 percent then that would mean the actual return on the investment is 11 percent after annualized tax returns.

SELLING MUTUAL FUND SHARES

To calculate your gain or loss you need to know the basis of those shares involved. If you sell all your shares at the same time it is easy to figure your basis, but if you sell only a portion of your fund, you need to determine the basis of your shares. One answer is to use average methods. If you decide not to use an averaging method, there is a three-step process to determine the basis of the particular shares you are selling. The process consists of determining which shares you sold, determining those shares' initial basis, and making any necessary adjustments to the basis. The Internal Revenue Service tax law says that when you sell shares of a mutual fund, what you are selling is the earliest shares that you originally acquired. The initial basis of shares is the original cost, and that includes any commission or load fees. It is possible for a mutual fund share basis to be adjusted. That would happen if the mutual fund pays a non-taxable capital dividend. Then the basis would be reduced by the amount of that dividend. The second way is when a mutual fund makes a capital gain allocation, without paying a dividend; the basis will be increased by 65 percent of this allocation. Many mutual funds do not pay this type of dividend.

If the investor chooses to go this way in finding an initial basis instead of using the averaging method, the investor should keep records that show each block of shares' purchased basis. If the investor buys shares under a savings plan and has dividends reinvested then the investor would need to keep a record of this as a block of shares. When averaging, this can eliminate many of the above calculations. The easiest averaging method is a single-category method. For many people this offers the best tax verdict. With this method the average basis of all shares the investor owns is equal to the basis of any share you sell. The basis is used to determine the gain or loss at the time of sale. The single-category method is the least flexible, but the easiest way to go. There are some mutual funds that are willing to do these calculations for the clients; the investor must meet requirements to be eligible to use this method. The investor must not maintain physical possession of his/her certificates of shares, they must be held in an account. Next, the investor must not have used a double-category method previously for the same fund. Third, if an investor has received any shares as a gift, then there may be additional eligibility requirements. After an averaging method is selected, the investor must stick with it for all transactions within that particular mutual fund.

SINGLE CATEGORY VERSUS DOUBLE CATEGORY

To use the single-category method, the basis of all shares will be added and divided by the number of shares involved. This average is the basis of the shares the investors has sold. In addition, it is important for an investor to know the time period in which the shares were owned. This way, the investor can sell the earliest shares that were purchased. This works out better since taxes are better with long-term gain versus short-term gain. Should there be any gift share involvement, there is a special rule. If the shares have a basis larger than their value at the time of the gift, the rule applies. The investor has to use the date of gift value, which is not the regular basis. From this, any loss on a sale will be determined, but the regular basis will be used to calculate a gain.

In preparing a tax return, for the first time after selling stock from a specific fund the investor would need to attach a statement to the return in electing an averaging method.

In reference to the double-category averaging method, it is more complicated than the single in that it may not bring the greatest results. With this method, the investor keeps track of the average basis of long-term shares in separation from the short-term shares. When the investor makes a sale there is a choice in the shares that are being sold, long-term or short-term. It is possible to save tax this way on particular sales, although if the investor cannot average the short-term and long-term shares the consequences could be more tax. The investor needs to know the basis of particular shares. There is greater flexibility for a tax benefit using this method. Meanwhile, if the investor has been purchasing shares for a while in a mutual fund that was in constant value increase then some of those shares could be sold shortly after a drop in value. By doing this, you can specify the selling of the short-term shares while having a short-term loss rather than a long-term gain. This means taxes would be lower. Using this method for a tax benefit often depends on the value of a mutual fund that is decreasing in value.

EXAMPLE

Pat bought shares at $200 a month for six months totaling $1,200. She had decided to sell her shares. If she decides to sell all of them, it is very easy to see that her basis would be $1,200. However, she is still uncertain she wants to sell everything. She finally decided to sell at least ten shares. The next step would be figuring how much the shares cost her and how much tax she would need to pay. The first purchase she made was for 3.10 shares. Her next purchase was 3.40 shares and her third purchase was 3.50 shares. This equals ten, which also suit the finals that would be sold. The reason she went back to the earliest shares is because the tax law requires this method of selling.

WEB SITES

InvestorsGuide
www.investorguide.com

IRS Tax Tips for Capital Gains and Losses
www.irs.gov

SmartMoney.com
www.smartmoney.com

CASE STUDY: T. RITSON FERGUSON

Chief Investment Officer/Managing Director of ING Real Estate Securities.

ING Clarion Real Estate Securities

201 King of Prussia Rd., Suite 600

Radnor, Pennsylvania 19087

www.ingclarion.com

http://www.ingclarion.com/INGClarion/Clarion+RE+Securities/

Phone: 888-711-4272

Fax: 610-996-2500

ING Real Estate is the world's largest real estate firm. The ING Clarion Real Estate Securities, L.P. (ING CRES) arm runs an approximate $21 billion out of $140 billion among the entire company. "ING CRES offers a variety of investment solutions including separate accounts, mutual funds, closed-end funds, and absolute return strategies." The company began managing its United States real estate portfolios in 1984 and due to an ever-changing trend began managing a global portfolio in 2001. Today, under the real estate securities portfolios there are five open-ended funds and two closed-ended funds. Since the funds are closed-ended, its shares are limited. Altogether, there are five different mutual funds.

In giving advice for investors, "A typical investor tends to think about real estate stocks as sensitive to interest rates because they pay high dividends. That's not the case necessarily. The real drivers are economic growth and the health of the real estate market. And those are the factor we focus on," said T. Ritson Ferguson, Chief Investment Officer of ING Clarion Real Estate Securities. ING Clarion Real Estate Securities' success is contributed to an excellent management team of different backgrounds and expertise that keep a portfolio going. All investors have certain objectives that need to be met, which explains why the company continues to launch funds that accommodate different tastes. Since 2004, foreign investment interest has really taken off and today global funds continue to be successful, as they tend to offer larger opportunities. Behind the scenes at ING, no matter what

CASE STUDY: T. RITSON FERGUSON

fund an investor may choose, it is all managed by the same team. Two closed-ended funds are the ING Clarion Global Real Estate Income Fund (NYSE: IGR) and the ING Clarion Real Estate Income Fund (NYSE:IIA). Using the closed-ended fund as an example, NYSE:IGR, there are roughly $3 billion in total assets. It is an income-oriented vehicle for global real estate investors and offers excellent liquidity via the NYSE. The dividend yield for this fund was 8.2 percent as of November 30, 2007 — not bad. Meanwhile, an open-ended mutual fund ING Global Real Estate A (IGLAX) is obviously another global investment but in relation to others, it is strong, receiving five star ratings from Morningstar.

The global and international portfolios account for approximately $18 billion of the $21 billion of ING Clarion Real Estate Securities' Assets Under Management (AUM). Ninety percent of this mutual fund is invested in stocks "principally engaged in the real estate industry", 2.47 percent in bonds while the remaining is invested in miscellaneous items. The top ten holdings (securities) include Simon Property Group, Inc., ProLogis Trust, Boston Properties, Inc., Mitsubishi Estate and more. To understand the bigger picture visit **http://finance.google.com/finance?client=ob&q=IGLAX**. As a member of ING Real Estate, ING CRES is a wholly owned subsidiary of ING Groep, N.V. (Netherlands).

Comparing Funds

ING CLARION GLOBAL REAL ESTATE INCOME FUND (AMEX:IGR)	
Funds Facts	
NYSE Symbol	IGR
NASDAQ Symbol	XIGRX
CUSIP	44982G104
Inception Date	02/24/2004
Inception NAV	14.33
Inception Share Price	15.00
Total Net Expense Ratio	1.07 percent*

ING CLARION GLOBAL REAL ESTATE INCOME FUND (AMEX:IGR)	
Fund Advisor	ING Clarion Real Estate Securities
Portfolio Manager	T. Ritson Ferguson
	Steve D. Burton
* RATIO OF EXPENSES TO AVERAGE DAILY MANAGED FUND ASSETS AS OF 12/31/06	

OBJECTIVE

"The Fund's primary objective is high current income. The Fund's secondary objective is capital appreciation. The Fund will invest substantially all but no less than 80 percent of its total assets in income-producing real estate securities (including REITs) located mainly in the developed markets of North America, Europe, Australia, and Asia. The fund can invest up to 25 percent of its assets in preferred shares of global real estate companies."

ING CLARION REAL ESTATE INCOME FUND (NYSE:IIA)	
Funds Facts	
NYSE Symbol	IIA
NASDAQ Symbol	XIIAX
CUSIP	449788108
Inception Date	09/25/2003
Inception NAV	14.32
Inception Share Price	15.00
Total Net Expense Ratio	1.08 percent*
Fund Advisor	ING Clarion Real Estate Securities
Portfolio Manager	T. Ritson Ferguson
	Joseph P. Smith

Ratio of expenses to average daily managed assets as of 12/31/06

OBJECTIVE

"The Fund's primary objective is high current income. The Fund's secondary objective is capital appreciation. Under normal market conditions, the Fund

ING CLARION REAL ESTATE INCOME FUND (NYSE:IIA)

Funds Facts

will invest at least 90 percent of its total assets in income-producing "Real Estate Securities." The Fund will invest at least 70 percent of its total assets in Real Estate Equity Securities and may invest up to 30 percent of its total assets in Real Estate Fixed Income Securities."

INTERNATIONAL FUND

Daily Prices (as of 12/21/2007)

Net Asset Value	$ Change	% Change	Previous	Offering Price	YTD
$12.60	+0.25	+2.02	$12.35	$13.37	-0.48%

Average Annual Total Returns

	YTD	1 YR	3 YR	5 YR	10 YR			
As of 11/30/2007 (Most Recent Month End)							Total	Net
At NAV	+6.39	+12.95	—	—	—	+20.67	2.01%	1.50%
With Load	+0.26	+6.42	—	—	—	+16.66		
As of 09/30/2007 (Most Recent Quarter End)								
At NAV	+10.54	+29.78	—	—	—	+26.08		
With Load	+4.17	+22.28	—	—	—	+21.46		
Current Maximum Sales Charge: 5.75%								

Average Annual Total Returns

"Includes Acquired Fund Fees and Expenses which are not fees or expenses incurred by the Funds directly. These fees and expenses include each Fund's pro rata share of the cumulative expenses charged by the Acquired Funds in which the Funds invest. The fees and expenses will vary based on each Fund's allocation of assets to, and the annualized net expenses of, the particular Acquired Funds.

"The Adviser has contractually agreed to limit expenses of the Fund. This agreement excludes interest, taxes, brokerage and extraordinary expenses, subject to possible recoupment within three years. The actual expenses of the Fund are in excess of the contractual expense limits and such expenses are being waived to the contractual cap. The expense limits will continue through at least March 1, 2008.

"It is important to note that the Fund has a limited operating history. Performance over a longer period of time may be more meaningful than short-term performance.

"Past performance is no guarantee of future results. The performance quoted represents past performance. Investment return and principal value of an investment will fluctuate, and shares, when redeemed, may be worth more or less than their original cost.

"SEC fund returns assume the reinvestment of dividends and capital gain distributions and include a sales charge. Net Asset Value fund returns assume the reinvestment of dividends and capital gain distributions but do not include a sales charge. Results would have been less favorable if the sales charge were included. Total return for less than one year is not annualized."

◄ CHAPTER 6 ►

The Safety of Online Investing

INVESTMENT SCAMS

Look out for ear candy. We never get everything we want, so the same goes when you are approached with an investment offer where everything seems perfect. There is always a catch to something right? Billions of dollars have been lost from investment scams. Aside from those people who do not have anything better to do giving cause to computer viruses, there are also online investment scams. Viruses and scams have really gotten bad. I personally do not open any e-mail where the sender's name is not recognized. There are shady Web sites in which they lure the investors to thinking a certain way, and then the investors end up losing money. The Web sites are very professional looking and are not in use for long, as the escape artists want to get away. They are in business just long enough to take your money, spend it, and get away without being caught.

BULLETINS & CHATROOMS

The same caution needs to stay with the investor on most bulletin boards, chat rooms, and other electronic resources, as those places are frankly freedom of speech boards where everyone is entitled to their opinion. For some fraudsters, the readers can be persuaded into believing things. It is important for the investor to become familiar with as much as possible with the stock markets, learning to recognize names that are reputable with good records of accomplishment and those that are not. There have been opportunities in which it is claimed the IRS or SEC supports a random investment, when in fact they do not. It is just to further entice the investor into believing something is safe and protected. Other scams that have risen are investment matchmaker business, in which a broker portrayed company will assist you in buying what fits your budget. When these companies do not have much information about them and want more information about you, including your Social Security and financial information, you should just run the other way. Often times, these sources do not disclose fee which you will be charged, as well as any negative background or conflicts of interest. Meanwhile, you have learned that the majority of stocks are not tax-free, and that your stock company's information can be found somewhere through the SEC. If by chance you find an investment ad in which it is a perfect investment, risk-free, tax-free, and confidential, you should beware.

BOILER ROOMS

Boiler rooms claim to be a broker or bank. The names usually sound like legitimate financial institutions. They are good at hard sales, meaning they push the investor to buy shares in companies that do not exist. Investors are lured into these rooms both by phone and online. The Web sites are usually high-tech, and they go as far as naming individuals with high educational degrees at well-known universities. However, the chances of finding a record of these people are very doubtful. There is also what is called "pump and dump" where touting of a company's stock takes place. The investor is tricked into buying cheap stocks where the price of those stocks is manipulated and then it dives, making the actually stock price dive and leaving the investor with nothing. Microcap companies are the usual players. Offers of this kind are often on message boards. There have been international investment bankers who guarantee risk-free bank notes that will bring excellent returns. "They can be offered in the form of arbitrage contracts, bank debentures, and other types of international currency trading contracts." (Price, 147). These things do not even exist. A lot of times, investment scams surround those risky penny stocks where the pink sheets (no SEC here) are involved. It is unfortunate that some people cannot contain themselves breaking laws and, in these cases, manipulating securities.

Some stock companies have even gone as far as manipulating the buying and selling of their stocks, which in turn convinces the investor that it is a popular stock and that there is a lot of trading taking place. It is your choice as always, but again, checking the SEC filings and EDGAR database is really the first step you should take before doing anything. You should also see where the scam artist is licensed (state) and the company's history. The more information you have, the better. Lawsuits, liens, and judgments are what you need to look for, as well as the date and time of the information. In an investment, you must obtain a copy of the prospectus as well as a financial statement of the company. If you are still uncertain, you should just check with a broker. Though we want to believe everything we read, those online newspaper and newsletters in which there is paid advertising may not entirely be true. The paper owners themselves survive on advertisements, so they do not particularly care and probably do not realize if there is an unethical advertisement in which untrue advice is being offered.

NAVIGATION SOFTWARE

In addition, security for the Internet in general has improved over the last few years, and having navigation software is your best bet offering the most security. This should have come with your computer, but is also downloadable at software sites. Anyone that owns a computer should know that there is software that exists that prevents cookies from being sent to a hard drive in which Internet activity is observed. This means any Web site visited can send a cookie to your computer in observation of other sites you have visited. Netscape is a familiar name that assists with this sort of thing.

EXAMPLE

Quite often, Ryan was receiving numerous e-mails. Because he was an investor, it seemed as though random companies had obtained his information somehow. There were several e-mails regarding penny stocks in which he was advised to invest. These e-mails were sent not from companies, but from individuals. The subject of the e-mails would sometimes be "non-word' meaning it would be some made up word. Struck with confusion, Ryan would open these e-mails and find advice on purchasing penny stocks or IPOs, but because the sources were random and shady, Ryan deleted the e-mails. Another example of these e-mails includes something that had subject headings such as "buy a birthday card." Ryan opened the e-mail only to be greeted by another offer of a similar nature. At first, Ryan tried to respond to the e-mails a couple of times to let these people know he was not interested, only to find that the address was phony or blocked. Should those e-mail addresses have worked and he took the advice, it could have been fraudulent information. This was a case however, where someone had too much time on his or her hands. Eventually, Ryan just deleted the odd e-mails without opening them, and then the e-mails quit coming.

NIGERIAN 419

Sometimes there are Nigerian 419 fraud incidents where investors have received e-mails from Nigeria where whoever is sending the e-mail wants to make use of an investor's bank accounts. What they do is request that you deposit large funds into a bank account, and in return the investor will receive a large percentage. The fraudsters then ask you to pay an upfront fee to release the money in the check account. While the whole thing is a total scam, there have been investors that have done this. There is a web site that provides more information. **www.419eater.com**

PYRAMIDS

State and Federal Securities Regulators can assist in observation of these types of scams. **www.sec.gov/ consumer/jtoptips.htm** That is not the end of it, beware of pyramid schemes. Most of us receive random e-mails (SPAM) occasionally and, in this case, e-mails are sent out in which you are asked to recruit a number of friends. Those friends are then asked to do the same, but during the entire process those involved buy pyramid products where stocks are involved. You are given a return for recruiting someone new. Those initial individuals expect they will reach the top of the pyramid, making the most of their first investment. Watch out for those ridiculous chain letters, too. Meanwhile, investment seminars are other online scams as you are expected to enroll via e-mail. Helpful observations in recognizing a possible scam are to identify signs of urgency and exceptional profits. If someone is trying to pressure you into an investment then take as much time as you want because this really is not a good sign. Fast money profits are not the way to go if those large return numbers are enough to make you question yourself. Always go with the first instinct.

FALSE LABELS AND LOGOS

Unfortunately, fraudsters have been known to copy original logos, documents, and anything else that could benefit them in tricking someone to go onto a fictitious Web site.

"Another trick involves the misuse of a regulator's seal. The fraudsters copy the official seal or logo from the regulator's website — or create a bogus seal for a fictitious entity — and then use that seal on documents or web pages to make the deal look legitimate. You should be aware that the SEC — like other state and federal regulators in the U.S. and around the world — does not allow private entities to use its seal. Moreover, the SEC does not "approve" or "endorse" any particular securities, issuers, products, services, professional credentials, firms, or individuals." **www.sec.gov**

INSIDER TRADING

Another form of fraud is insider trading is when management in a company has information about that particular company that the general public does not know. These people can actually use this information to buy or sell stock in their favor, but it is illegal. This describes the Enron case, Martha Stuart issue, and Michael Milken, a greedy Wall Street bond broker.

Milken is believed to have caused the SEC to tighten laws after this incident happened in the 80s although that would not seem apparent after the Enron scandal. Milkens specialty was junk bonds developing high-yield debt, later causing major problems for many corporations.

In 1989 Milken was charged with nearly 100 accounts of racketeering in addition to securities fraud. Racketing is the epitome of crime in that is organized in a way where money is demanded from these businesses, or else. In 1975, a Racketeer Influenced and Corrupt Organizations Act was formed to prevent this. This man was guilty al right of securities fraud as he repeatedly manipulated investments. Although he was sent to serve ten years in prison, he got out in two, and was still considered one of the richest men in America. He's not on Donald's level though. In 2003, Martha Stewart got busted. One would think those that bake and decorate are not white-collar thieves, but apparently, it happens. After obtaining an insider secret, a complaint was filed that Stewart sold stock in a biopharmaceutical company, ImClone Systems, Inc. back in 2001. It was alleged that Stewart and Bacanovic had created an alibi although under an investigation some thinks were kept concealed. The SEC was also on top of things The Commission alleges that Stewart and Bacanovic went on to lie when the Commission staff and criminal authorities questioned them about the facts surrounding Stewart's sale of ImClone stock. Stewart and Bacanovic fabricated an alibi for Stewart's trades, stating that she sold her ImClone stock because she and Bacanovic had decided earlier that she would sell if ImClone's stock price fell below $60 per share. In addition, Stewart told the government that she did not recall anyone telling her that day that any of the Waksals were selling their ImClone stock.

CHAPTER 7

Brokers and Financial Advisors

I mentioned earlier that it is difficult for the new investor to learn to trust a stranger with money. It is wise to do the research on an individual because you do not want to learn the hard way. That is not to say that everyone is perfect. An Investment Advisors Act was passed in 1940 requiring any advisor to register with the SEC. This includes any person or organization that offers advice for a fee. A form known as ADV part II is necessary to file, which you as an investor should be able to locate as by law; your broker or other advisor should release this to you upon request. This form will allow you to view any negative information brought against that person.

You can call a broker an advisor or an advisor a broker, it is up to you. You can check to see if both are licensed, in addition to any other negative points if they exist. A financial advisor helps you with your financial goals as does a broker. They can point you in the direction on what is the best way to go in making an investment, whether it is buying a home or investing in stocks. They are more for long-term commitment planning. There is a Certified Financial Planning Board that certifies individuals to do this. There are also certified financial planners and fee-based management consultants. They all charge a fee, but they vary slightly as they have different duties. A broker helps you with the buying and selling of stock. An advisor can do this also, but they also have tax guidance, insurance knowledge, and trust help aside from the regular investing.

With an online broker, a good broker will call you occasionally just to find out if there is anything that you want to change, or he may have suggestions to get rid of something or buy something else. Everything must be done with your approval. Depending on how active you are in your investing, brokers will keep different amounts of contact. Some brokers send birthday cards and holiday cards, so they do work with you on a personable level while remaining professional. There are many full service firms with online sites. Examples include *Ameritrade*, *AG Edwards*, and *Fidelity*. There are families of mutual funds that can be purchased without broker fees, but if you use their brokers to purchase individual stocks, for example, they will charge a commission, which can be expensive. Another way of trading is with a company such as *Scottrade*, *Etrade*, and *Ameritrade*, who charge minimal commissions because you do not really have any dealing with a broker, you just do everything yourself online within that Web site. With *AG Edwards*, a stockbroker company would charge full commission on certain purchases, higher than most. *AG Edwards* may charge something like $40 a year as an investor fee. At times there are some mutual funds you can sell without commission fees and others where there is a due to be paid. In trading fees, *Merrill Lynch* or *Smith Barney*, for example, may charge an annual fee somewhere in the range of $1500 to $1700 annually to manage your assets while making an unlimited amount of trades.

When you open your online account, you have to fill out an application form. This can be done online. Sometimes broker firms such as *Scottrade* can assign you to a local branch where you can mail this information. This is an SEC requirement and also proof that your broker is aware of your financial status in the pursuit of proper management. There are different ways of sending money to your advisor. You can take it to the local branch, send a check or money order to the online address, or transfer money from a checking account. This process can take just a few minutes or a few weeks to get everything going. You cannot have a joint account unless you have a spouse, but you can choose from an individual, custodial, trust, corporate, IRA, or retirement account. You can have more than one account. Sometimes brokers will assist you with a new account with a catch of no initial deposit. Once you begin depositing money or securities, that broker will then get commission.

FULL SERVICE

A full-service brokerage is one that has the full package. The research is done, investment advice is given and the market data is done. Brokers are assigned to investors and will occasionally contact the investor with changes and/ or idea and should regularly do so with any investment move. This would mean it is a tag-team effort as you do have some say in what goes on. The fees for this type of investment are often higher.

DISCOUNT BROKERS

They are great for online investing. This way you can make all your decisions and through an online brokerage firm. In this situation, the investor places an order in which the firm then executed the trade. These firms still offer research and advice while all feels are substantially less.

RECOGNIZING A BAD BROKER

There is a Central Registration Depository where brokers and brokerages are listed as licensed. This information is available at the National Association of Securities Dealers web site. Do not forget that the NYSE also releases information on disciplinary actions.

Your state regulator Web site will also help in making the decision about your broker. A good broker will not only educate you on investing but will also let you ask as many questions necessary to better assist you. A bad broker would most likely distract you by avoiding certain questions, causing you to become sidetracked. The first question on your part should be company background information, track records, meeting others within that particular firm, and references. If a broker is freaked out by any of this, then that is a first sign of a bad or dishonest broker since it might be the case that there is reason to hide something.

Other questions that bring hesitance might include copies of a stock company's prospectus as well as information on the company's stance with a regulatory agency or any other financial disclosure. This is also the sign that your investments are not protected. If at some point you are ready to cash out your investment and it seems as though your broker has an issue with this, this could be a bad sign. It is always good to try to get a written explanation about your investment directions; should there be a fraud case you will have evidence. Since good brokers seem to be on top of things while making you aware of every thought out move, a broker that seems hesitant to meet with you or discuss things is another sign of a bad broker. It is always wise to make observations of what your broker is doing when making a trade. There has been case where investors become lazy with the notion that "my broker knows what he is doing and he will take care of it." This is fine, and things could be looking good for a while for your investment portfolio. Depending on the situation, a broker could be making a commission on virtually several trades. You would not care as long as it is beneficial to you, but do nor wait until you have lost several thousand dollars because your broker was more focused on making commission than on making the right moves. In any case though, that is another sign of a bad broker. It is important that you open your investment statements regularly while doing market comparisons, even when you have a broker. Anytime you are uncertain about anything, ask your broker what it means. After all, that is what they are there for.

Note: Sometime those "small" investment firms may be charging a low commission. There are hidden costs in which they also make money off the asking and bidding price (spread).

TRACK RECORDS

The investor should keep in mind that brokers are just another word for a high-class salesperson. A living is made on primarily on commissions generated from orders to buy or sell. It is never a bad thing if you have doubts about a broker and your comfort level is just not there. The overall duties or everyday routine of the average broker is to research stocks and stay abreast of the latest financial news. What you have to determine is whether the research that is provided is credible and reliable. This is why a record of accomplishment is important, because no one knows whether a broker is experienced. In an initial consultation with a broker, the investor should ask as many questions as possible regarding not only the firm's background, but the brokers too.

WHEN RESEARCHING BROKERS OR BROKERAGES, LOOK FOR THE FOLLOWING:

Felony charges

Convictions

Written consumer complaints

Outstanding judgments or liens

Civil judgments

Work history

Criminal charges

Bond company denials

Criminal charges

Terminations

COSTS OF ONLINE BROKERAGE FIRMS

Sometimes people forget to tell you, or you overlook the smaller text in a contract regarding fees. This also applies to online investments, as there is often a cost associated with an online broker.

Just as there as there are different categories for stocks, the same applies to brokers. A full-service broker typically charges $20 and more for trades between 100 and 500. A discount broker offers the same in the range of $15 and $19.95, while a deep-discount broker would mean the same for only $14.95. Certain numbers are meant to be psychological, as $14.99 would naturally seem better than $15. In most cases, investors keep their stashes in money market accounts until an investment is made. Where there is an online broker, there is an online deposit fee. The minimum fee is $2000, and the rest would depend on the brokerage. Commission can also be deviant in that even the smallest payment to a broker could actually cost you more. Commission rates can vary widely amongst brokerages. Most of the time these rates are valued by the number of shares traded, price, and the amount of money that has been invested. Whatever the fee, the amount is worth it as long as the outcome is good. Commission rates are one of the most important questions, too. There should be no beating around the bush. If the broker and brokerage seem to meet all your needs, then it is your decision in taking the next step. Should you have any discrepancies or a bad experience, brokers are fully aware of the SEC, which you can go to if there is an unfairness issue. Before 1975, commission was fixed, but today they are negotiable.

CASE STUDY: JODY HAMPTON

INVESTMENT BROKER

Wachovia Securities, LLC

50 Old Courthouse Square

Suite 110

Santa Rosa, CA 95404

Jody.hampton@agedwards.com

"The stock market runs on two things, fear and greed," said Jody Hampton, an investment broker from the former AG Edwards. I decided to do an interviewwith your everyday broker having nothing to do with online broker investing. In doing the interview with Hampton, the process was going smoothly until he looked at me and said "I have a client." Apparently, this broker was serious when it came to business. A 15-minute, scheduled interview had been cut short by an important client.

"Clients first is philosophy, brokers second, and the firm third," said Hampton

I made observation that he was the only broker left in the former AG Edwards office. All of the other brokers had quit and went with the manager and he was the only one that stayed behind. I assumed there was an awfully good reason for this. According to Hampton, he obtained 5,000 additional client accounts, compounded with 6,000 he already had, due to other broker resignations. There where at least ten offices, and not one of them had a broker in it, except for Hampton. The phones were silent; the building quiet and there was one secretary.

On a lighter note, the latest news about the firm is a merger with a well-known and established firm by the name of Wachovia Securities. Wachovia

CASE STUDY: JODY HAMPTON

is a large bank that has acquired firms such as Prudential and others in addition to world savings. Since AG and Wachovia have merged, there will be a lot more services offered that could not be done before. If AG Edwards has a bank backing it, then more information will be readily available at the brokers' fingertips. Currently, Wachovia brings 5 different venues of trading stocks. In October 2007, this merger became official. Wachovia now serves as the nation's second largest firm.

The company is comprised of more than $1 trillion in "client assets," and more than 15,000 standbys waiting to help. There are over 3,300 broker office locations for Wachovia in addition to approximately 1,500 stand-alones.

"As a result of the merger, A.G. Edwards shareholders will receive 0.9844 shares of Wachovia common stock and $35.80 in cash for each share of their A.G. Edwards common shares. Shareholders may access additional information at Wachovia's Investor Relations Web site, wachovia.com/investor. The site provides access to the most current news and financial information on Wachovia." **www.wachovia.com**

Smart Money, **www.smartmoney.com/broker/yourselfr/index.cfm?story=.** Interestingly enough, most clients of AG Edwards in the Santa Rosa, California did not ask questions. They all just went with the flow with expectations to reap new benefits. A few clients left AG Edwards because they didn't like the idea of a bank. And ironically in the shift, many clients fired their brokers, but stayed with AG Edwards. There is no explanation for this. Ultimately, my favorite part of the interview was when Hampton admitted that it is much cheaper for investors to do the work online. While AG has many analysts, trading stock online does not cost as much. "I can't get the stock as cheap as they can get it online because of my commission stock," Hampton said. A common theme viewed by brokers is that "people always buy stock for the wrong reason." Since people that trade stocks, in a trade, use most online services people often make mistakes with the wrong decisions. Hampton said "For every trader that drives a Mercedes, there is someone that will park their car and put their gas in it for them."

Offline brokers work more with investors.

The best advice I can share, Hampton said people do not realize they are

CASE STUDY: JODY HAMPTON

becoming an actual owner of a company when purchasing stock. And people need to know that investing is not necessarily a get-rich-quick thing. Equities (stocks) outperform all assets over time. They can be extremely volatile in the short-term and clients need to understand that. A lot of people do not see this. "Reinvesting dividends is the best thing you can do," Hampton said. Again, dividends come from the company earnings and really have nothing to do with the earnings.

"A portfolio is a lot like a snowball, the more you handle it, the smaller it gets," Hampton said.

www.wachovia.com

It is normal for a broker to ask you about your investment experience, as they have to determine what investment is best for you. If you already have other accounts elsewhere, that broker may try and convince you to move to their firm. That is in your hands. Investment objectives for a broker include reviewing capital preservation growth, and your current income. This is all done to help the broker in making decisions.

Yahoo.com provides a list of licensed brokers at:

dir.yahoo.com/Business_and_Economy/Shopping_and_Services/ Financial_Services/Investment_Services/Brokerages/Internet_Trading.

Smart Money, www.smartmoney.com/broker/yourselfr/index.cfm?story=.

OVER 5 TRADES A WEEK:	
A.B. Watley	**www.abwatley.com**
Ameritrade	**www.ameritrade.com**
BrownCo	**www.brownco.com**
Scottrade	**www.scottrade.com**

FOR THOSE THAT LOVE THE INTERNET AND CHECKING INVESTMENTS:	
Fidelity	**www.fidelity.com**
Merrill Lynch Direct	**www.mldirect.ml.com**
Charles Schwab	**www.schwab.com**

TRACK RECORD SITES:	
Federal Trade Commission	www.ftc.gov
National Association of Securities Dealers	www.nasdr.com
Securities and Exchange Commission	www.sec.gov
	www.Abika.com
North American Securities Administrators Association	www.nasaa.org

BROKERS & BROKERAGES:	
Abby Sharedealing	www.abbeysharedealing.com
AB Watley	www.abwatley.com
Accutrade	www.accutrade.com
Active Investor	www.preftech.com
AG Edwards	www.agedwards.com
Alaron Trading	www.alarontrading.com
American Express Financial District	www.american.express.com
Ameritrade	www.ameritrade.com
Atlantic Financial	www.af.com
Barclays Stockbrokers	www.barclays-stockbroker.co.uk
BCL Online	www.bclnet.com
Bidwell	www.bidwell.com
Brown & Co.	www.brownco.com
Bull and Bear	www.bullbear.com
Charles Schwab	www.schwab.com
Citicorp Investments	www.citicorp.com
CompuTel	www.rapidtrade.com
Datek Online	www.datek.com
Discover Brokerage Direct	www.discoverbrokerage.com
DLJdirect	www.dljdirect.com
Dreyfus	www.dreyfus
E*Trade	www.etrade.com

BROKERS & BROKERAGES:	
Empire Financial	www.lowfees.com
FarSight Financial Services	www.farsight.com
Fastrade	www.fastrade.co.uk
Fidelity	www.fidelity.com
Firstrade.com	www.firsttrade.com
ForbesNet	www.forbesnet.com
Fleet Brokerage	www.fleet.com
Freedom Investments	www.freedominvestments.com
Freeman Welwood	www.freemanwelwood.com
Friedman Billings Ramsey	www.fbr.com
GFN Investments	www.gfn.com
GRO Corporation	www.grotrader.com
Internet Trading	www.internettrading.com
Investex Securities Group	www.investexpress.com
Investrade	www.investrade.com
Jack Carl Futures	www.jackcarl.com
James Brearly & Sons	www.jbrearly.co.uk
JB Oxford	www.jboxford.com
J.P. Morgan	www.jpmorgan.com
LFG Linnco Futures Group	www.lfgllc.com
Lind-Waldock	www.lind-waldock.com
Linder Funds	www.linderfunds.com
Livetrade	www.livetrade.com
Lombard Institutional Brokerage	www.lombard.com
Main Street Market	www.mainstmarket.com
MB Trading	www.mbtrading.com
Merrill Lynch	www.merilllynch.com
Morgan Stanley Dean Witter	www.online.msdw.com
Mr. Stock	www.mrstock.com
Muriel Siebert & Co., Inc.	www.siebertnet.com
My Discount Broker	www.mydiscountbroker.com

BROKERS & BROKERAGES:	
National Discount Brokers	www.ndb.com
Newport Discount	www.newport-discount.com
Pacific Brokerage Services	www.tradepbs.com
Paine Weber	www.painewebber.com
PAWWS Financial Network	www.pawws.com
Peremel Online	www.peremel.com
Preferred Trade	www.preftech.com
Prudential Securities	www.prusec.com
Quick & Reilly Online	www.ndb.com
SAI Advisors, Inc.	www.on-lineinvest.com
Saloman Smith Barney	www.smithbarney.com
Schwab	www.schwab.com
Scottsdale Securites	www.scottstrade.com
Scottrade	www.scottrade.com
Siebert, Muriel	www.msiebert.com
Smith Barney	www.smithbarney.com
Stocks4Less	www.stock4less.com
SureTrade	www.suretrade.com
TD Waterhouse Securities Inc.	www.waterhouse.com
Thomas F. White	www.tfwhite.com
TradeOptions	www.tradeoptions.com
Tradestar Investments	www.tradestar.com
Tradewell Discount Investing	www.trade-well.com
Trading Direct	www.tradingdirect.com
TruTrade	www.trutrade.com
Wall Street Access	www.wsaccess.com
Wall Street Discount Corporation	www.wsdc.com
Wang Investments	www.wangvest.com
Waterhouse Securities	www.waterhouse.com
Web Street Securities	www.webstreetsecurities.com
Wilshire Capital Management	www.wilshirecm.com

BROKERS & BROKERAGES:	
Wit Capital Group Inc.	www.witcapital.com
Wyse Securities	www.wyse-sec.com
W.R. Hambrecht	www.wrhambrecht.com
York Securities	www.tradingdirect.com
ZAP Futures	www.zapfutures.com
Ziegler Thrift	www.ziegler.com

Those who are Internet savvy may be into researching the research. There are Web sites, which assist with comparing brokerages to brokerages. These sites may look over all the possible candidates in detail while coming up with a comparison and a score, ranking the best one first. These research services compare costs, customer statistics, and many other things for the investors' best interest. All of these searches can cater to an investor's specific questions and the answers are based on investor profiles. By doing all this, the investor can often see the strengths and weakness among brokers.

WEB SITES

www.gomez.com

www.epinions.com

www.consumersearch.com

www.winzy.com

www.redbooktrucking.com

www.ticketbrokerratings.com

forexadvisor.us

Note: A Bankerage is Not a Brokerage

It is possible for you do accomplish this and much more using an online bankerage.

Since 1999 financial institutions have been able to combine brokerage and banking services. This is of great benefit to investors by being able to see all accounts in one place. It gives the opportunity to gather information about financial situations without having to move back and forth between a brokerage and a bank. Investors may have checking and saving accounts, bill paying services, brokerage services, an equity line of credit, all on one monthly statement. Mutual fund management and brokerage fees are usually low and high quality research is offered. Some bankerages offer free ATM service, higher yields on CDs and good rates on interest bearing checking accounts. Studies done by Corporate Insight show financial institutions are not using the Web as much as they could be to offer their clients all possible benefits. Corporate Insight monitors 18 brokerages and claims that only 40 percent can be considered a full "bankerage." This term has been coined as being a brokerage that offers FDIC insured checking and savings accounts, plus any other usual banking tools, and can be accessed through a single web site. Citibank, Netbank, Wells Fargo, and Fidelity are among the major online bankerages.

◄ CHAPTER 8 ►

Finding Your Investment Style

Most first-time investors would naturally feel overwhelmed with trying to learn the stock market: where to invest, when, and how. Your investment style should lay out your goals depending on if you are conservative, aggressive, or anywhere in between. Your financial status is obviously a main factor, but your goals determine your style. The conservative investors are those who are not in for losing any money or would hope not anyway. If there is $3000 going, in the end that much is expected to come out and then some. These investors are good for short-term money market accounts, common stocks, and bonds. Money-market funds are not protected by the FDIC or the SEC. If you have money to lose, or you are very free-spirited, then you may be willing to take the risk and invest aggressively. These investors are out to make money, and they want to do it fast, whereas the conservatives are a little more cool, calm, and collected and have the time to sit back and relax. Aggressive investors tend to have more money and gain greater returns. Money being lost is never the hoped-for goal but it is not as important. If this does not apply, then the investor is somewhere in the middle. That means you like to take risks but can be rational, too. Someone that is conservative would be a nickel machine slot player while aggressive folks are throwing out $100 bills. Either way, money can be won. The middle of the road investor has the best of both worlds or is all over the casino with a bucket and a fat pocket. Conservative is ideally for those college students who just graduated, have a new job, and are still broke from the college bill. Anyone in his or her twenties and in this situation is most likely conservative, and it is not by choice. However, this is a good time to start saving for retirement, especially since there is news from the Social Security Administration that those benefits will most likely, not exist by the time retirement is reached. In other matters, diversification should not really be questionable; it is nearly a requirement for surviving in investments. There are several different ways you can determine your style, you can be passive or active in combination with growth and value choices. This is where the P/E ratio comes in again. Those investments or companies that are expected to expand more are in for the long run. Value investors are like people that read all the different price tag labels for the mustard choices at the grocery stories. There is nothing wrong with that. These investors also look for the cheaper stocks at the end of their business cycles. Active investors are like the aggressive while the passive are the more conservative. Active investors try to outdo and be on top of the market while the passive are in it for the long run.

CAPITAL GAINS & LOSSES

The difference between how much you sell or buy a stock represents a capital gain. A basis of this is usually the purchase price plus the commission charge by a broker. Short-term capital gains are held less than a year while long-term are more than a year. The long-term capital gains are taxed at a lower rate than ordinary income. With capital losses, the investor sells at a lower price than the purchase price. This loss can be deducted from income taxes. Investors can deduct up to $3,000 per year and if there is more loss than that, this loss may be carried over to the next year so if there is a $5,000 loss, only $3,000 could be deducted and the remaining $2,000 could hang around until the following tax year. When or if the price of an asset declines instead of appreciates, then this is a loss. If an investor gains and loses money in the same year, taxable income can actually be reduced as the numbers counteract one another.

"When a loss is carried over, it retains is character as long term or short term, as applicable. A long-term capital loss carried to the next tax year will reduce long-term capital gains (if any) actually realized during that year before being used to reduce that year's short-term capital gains (if any). If part of the loss is still unused, the taxpayer may carry it over to later years until it is completely used up, or until the death of the individual who incurred the loss. Generally, appreciated capital assets sold by an individual after being held more than one year (long-term capital gain) will be taxed at a maximum rate of 15%. For taxpayers earning less than $15,000 annually the tax rate on long-term capital gains is only 5% and will be 0% after 2008. For the sale of collectibles and small business stock, the rate of taxation for individuals is a maximum of 28%. Appreciated capital assets that are sold by individuals after being held less than one year (short-term capital gain) will be taxed as **ordinary income**, which rises as high as 39.6% in the U.S. progressive tax system.[1] Capital gains by entities taxed as corporations do not receive preferential treatment, and are taxed at a maximum rate of 35 percent.[2]"

www.sec.gov

SHORT SELLING

Some may call short selling naked selling because your butt is not covered. Short selling with stock is when you sell the stock you have with the intentions of repurchasing it a later date at a cheaper price. When a stock is expected to decline quite a bit, people do this in hopes that it will decrease. When this happens, you are actually borrowing a stock through a brokerage where there is another investor who also has the intentions of selling that stock in the market. You do not actually own the stock at this point in time. After you buy the stock at a cheaper price, as soon as it goes back up the investor can resell it at a profit. A short seller can buy a call option, an insurance policy in case the stock increases in value instead of decrease. If the stock increases, then the investor would lose money if a call option had not been purchased. The average buyer would not do this type of practice of buying short since the investor has to be very aware of market trends while studying stock prices. Assuming all goes well, your profit is a difference between what you received in selling the borrowed stock and what you paid to buy the shares back at a lower price. A stock can keep going up unless there is a stop-loss order. If this action does not take place, then that investor would lose everything originally invested. Since you borrowed the stock, you have borrowed the money, which must be paid back, plus a commission. This is a way to make money, but it is risky and you have to know what you are doing and are able to back up your loss. Considering you are borrowing money in the first place, it would not be a wise move for the first-time investor. If you borrow so much money and the stock increase then you still have to pay the amount borrowed plus what would actually be increased since the investor will owe more than what was originally borrowed.

EXAMPLE

Spike wanted to invest in a clothing company by the name of Hyre. Statistics showed that the stock price was steadily declining. He decided to buy short and having dealt with his stockbroker for many years, he knew that the broker would take a chance on this type of investment. He had cash in his account in which he bought 100 shares at $100 per share totaling $10,000 borrowed. This money was removed from his account and all of the shares were borrowed from another investor who owned 100 shares of the Hyre Company. Two weeks after this transaction, the shares of Hyre dropped to $90. Spike then put in an order to buy, which is "covering *your short." The broker then returned the money he borrowed plus the profit minus the commission, leaving Spike with more money for future investments. Spike was able to return the original $10,000 while making a profit of approximately $1,000.*

MARGIN ACCOUNTS

When the investor is not up to opening a cash account, a margin account is when you "buy on margin." But in this case you borrow money from the broker and the investor matches it with an amount that the investor can invest. Once this is accomplished there is twice as much buying power, and the initial investment will fluctuate with stock changes. The outcome is good if the price goes up because the investor has been able to purchase and sell more stock than the investor originally had money for. However, if the stocks go down you will lose money. You can either make twice as much profit or lose twice as much, so it is obviously risky. At a starting point, you own 50 percent of the investment and the broker owns 50 percent. When the stock goes up, your interest also goes up. And when the stock goes down, so does the investor's interest. That said, cashing out would mean more money would be owed to the broker, and the investor would lose part of the original allocation. While paying interest at the current rate to the brokerage, the condition is to plan for enough profit so that you will offset the borrowing costs. If you are in this position and a stock drops drastically then your stock is then undermargined. The brokerage will not be able to back the investor up which sets off a margin call. This is when you are required to throw in additional cash or securities.

The required amount to start a margin account is $2,000.

EXAMPLE

Joseph Augustus wanted to buy stock and he only had $2,000 to invest for a specific stock. He opened a margin account and added another $2,000, which was provided from a brokerage. He bought 40 shares of a company at $100 a share, of which he owned 50 percent. One of two things can happen to him. The stock can go up, as an example $10 per share. If he sold, the investment would be worth $4,400 leaving his margin of profit at $400. The other possibility that could happen to him would be that the stock drops $10 per share, in which case he would owe the brokerage money. If the percentage of loss drops below 35 percent he gets a margin call and has to add either cash or securities to the original amount borrowed. It is important that he meets the call immediately, since the broker can sell without notifying him. If that happens, the account will freeze, leaving Joe unable to do anymore trading within the account. Not all stocks can be bought on margin; it depends on the company.

Margin accounts are kind of strange because the investor can purchase more shares than there are readily available through a broker. The scary thing is if an investor buys a bunch of stock and those shares decrease drastically, the actual loan of the investor would have to be paid back – all at once. This means do not let you eyes oversell your mouth. Keep in mind also, that when an advisor sees a risk with these stocks, they do not have the time to call you on the phone to tell you to "look out."

WEB SITES

www.aaii.com

www.advisorinsight.com

www.barchart.com

www.b4utrade.com

www.businessweek.com

www.cbs.marketwatch.com

www.clearstations.com

www.equitymodel.com

www.estrong.com

www.fidelity.com

www.idayo.com

www.incrediblecharts.com

www.investors.com

www.investor.reuters.com

www.marketscreen.com

www.moneycentral.msn.com

www.morningstar.com

www.my.zacks.com

www.nasdaq.com

www.pristine.com

www.quicken.com

www.screen.yahoo.com

www.smartmoney.com

www.sixer.com

www.stockworm.com

www.tdwaterhouse.com

www.troweprice.com

www.valuengine.com

www.wallstreetcity.com

And those stocks that are under the radar are one of thousands of equities that are publicly traded. Sure the prospectuses are available, but with that many choices, who has time to go through it all? This is where screening seems extremely relevant.

With spread betting, the investor can trade on stocks in an effort to make bets on future products among a certain company. This also includes underlying cash products. Small amounts of money are committed in the OTC market. A middleman who issues the bet is the counterparty. Bets are truly based on a belief that a stock is expected to increase while interest rates will change, too. While the investor is trading on movements, a margin is in place in the 10 percent to 15 percent of the underlying value. No one can really advise you on how to place these spreads, no more than a broker could. People research information and go with the instincts. There are companies such as Cantor Index, which specializes in the assistance of spread betting. The company is worldwide making catering options even more to the investor with all opportunities including stocks, bonds, shares, indices and commodities. The company has been in existence for nearly six decades. The advantage of this range of betting is that there are no commission charges as there are with brokers in addition to fees. And everyone likes to hear when there is a tax-free move involved. The investment strategy is often a sell-short or buy-long option in which the investors' situation becomes a win-win one. What is unique about spread betting is such that investments are made to whatever type of share, but it is never really owned by the individual. By this you are buying or selling a "quote." This quote is based upon what the individual's bet is on and whether that asset will rise or fall. This is a leveraging investment in that the profits increase significantly when that spread bet is, right on the money. Cantor Index has different opportunities for different investors. The moral of the story is to keep in mind that spread betting can be high-risk. An initial investment is only a small percentage of what could become a large win.

Since these bets can be made internationally, US stocks and UK stocks can both be commingled among each other via American Depository Receipts. Visit **www.cantorindex. co.uk** for more information.

OPTIONS

An option may be considered an alternative investment. When an option is involved, there is a contract between a buyer and a seller. Not all online investment brokerages will offer option investments. Those that do will charge a contract commission fee or a flat fee. The whole purpose in buying an option contract is so that investors can position themselves in an instance where there will be a big change in the market. The contract will state that the buying or selling of shares. This is known as underlying stock and nothing in the contract states that the investor must buy or sell the stock. Contracts of this type include around 100 shares. Call and puts are two types of options. These contracts are in a 1 to nine-month time frame. Investors small or large turn to option contracts because it enables them to leverage their investment bringing nicer returns. A put-call ratio decreases when there are more buyers of calls than puts with an equity. When this ratio is high, more call buyers may emerge and the market will begin increasing. When interest rates are declining with the economy, options tend to be more expensive because investors tend to withdraw from their deposit accounts. Differences from options include *covered warrants* and *conventional warrants*. While options mean contract involvement, covered warrants do not. Covered warrants are more expensive than options. With a call option, an investor can purchase a specific number of shares at a specified price within a specific time period. The good news comes when the stock is above the agreed upon price in the contract. This is the goal of everyone. And with a put option, the contract assumes the holder the right to sell those 100 shares of stock at or before that date of expiration.

These investment strategies are more popular in Europe between the London Stock Exchange and the UK. The way it works is that the investor pays out a small premium. The investor may then buy or sell his/her assets. These covered warrants may be divided among calls and puts. This would actually make the investment less valuable. The difference compared to spread betting is that no more than 100 percent of the money can be lost. Meanwhile a conventional warrant is "used to buy a specified number of new shares in a company at a specified exercise price either at a given time, or within a given period." Warrants like these are not included in a balance sheet. That said, the same rights are not available and they are not includes as a companies share.

WEB SITES

INO.com

Quotes.ino.com

Chicago Board Options Exchange
www.cboe.com/delayquote/quotable.aspx

Philadelphia Stock Exchange
www.phlx.com

U.S. Futures and Options
www.site-by-site.com/usa/optfut.htm

Covered Calls
www.coveredcalls.com

OptionSmart
www.optionsmart.com

Options Industry Council
Pic.theocc.com/default.jsp

PitNews.com
www.pitnews.com

SchaeffersResearch.com
www.schaeffersresearch.com

optionsExpress
www.optionsexpress.com

PowerOptions
www.poweropt.com

Options Industry Council
www.optionscentral.com/desk/options_calc.jsp

◄ CHAPTER 9 ►

Chart Matters

A big part of the investment world includes charts and graphs. It suits some well, while others are challenged. Typically, investment graphs can be found everywhere on the Internet since they are used to show performance by either days, weeks, hours, and even years recording history. Maybe history was not your favorite class, but this is a different kind and it is necessary with this class. For those who work with a broker, graphs and charts are plentiful, and they are included with the commission charge. The software programs mentioned in Chapter 8 have tutorial advantage over these tools, making it easier to read on a computer screen one way or another via different spreadsheets and text files. Charts can show a company's financial status, investments by decades, averages, money flows, and strengths. Moving averages include the average price of a stock over a certain period. Since stocks stay either ahead or behind a moving average, it is easy to record movements foreshadowing gains or losses in the investment world. For some, it is simply easier to read a chart than to thimble through company paperwork. In the olden days, investors used to have to pay to preview charts. It was another way for people to make money. The Internet changed this as information became readily available at peoples' fingertips. It was not until the mid-1990s that stuff became free since there were more subscriptions to have the privilege of using charts than there was free information. Charting services as early as the 1990s could cost investors hundreds a month — and they paid. Keep in mind that free things may not be high quality. That does not apply to everything, but sometimes you pay more to get better service, so it is important to look into what company it is you are working with, as the charts may or may not be too accurate. The Internet also made charting easier with its advancement, as there was a time when all this data was entered via hand. Charts are generally easy to read and can be compared to others assisting in decisions that mean a fortune. Charts are also good in trend-spotting. It helps some decide if they should make an investment on the condition that a stock may rise or fall. Commodity investors are highly dependent on this tool. Although this is the last chapter, it could not go without saying there are several options in the chart selections, too. Everything is so plentiful these days.

Patterns show price fluctuations, trends, and struggles in the market. It means something is going on and it is the reader's job to figure out why. It mimics the trend of supply and demand. Some analyses include using charts to predict the future. The main things to keep in mind when observing charts are time frames, objectives, price performances, growth, history, price indicators, and moving averages. Settings can be changed in some instances.

BENCHMARKS

Benchmarking is also another good reason to keep a chart. They are used to evaluate the performance of a stock while comparing the performance of other stocks. Many of the software programs use a benchmark, but every company has a set benchmark as a reached (or unreached) goal mark. If the stock is not reaching that peak then new scenarios can be created. It can be looked at as a tool, referencing measurement. Another way to look at the benchmarks is "ways in which investors can set a challenge and reach it." With investment portfolios, benchmarking is primarily used to make comparisons among indexes such as the Russell 2000, NASDAQ Composite, and S&P 500. With charts, comparisons do not have to be observed every day but in enough time, on a monthly basis. If the investor's goal is not being reached, then it is time to crank up the game. Think logically and be sure to compare your stocks to others of similar nature. It is just not wise to compare a mouse to an elephant. Many of our domestic pension funds compare the real estate portfolios to the Lehman aggregate. It is viewed at a "broad bond market" index in addition to the S&P 500. Those investors that are more aggressive would vie that of NASDAQ or Russell 2000. Pension funds and sharks usually view these indexes annually, measuring performance. From this, it is observed where shifts can be made in the investment portfolios. Patterns will represent area where poor or positive performances exist. Benchmarks are measured annually although three to five years is sufficient to some because advisors, stocks and funds can be credited as good for the long-term investors. It is not always a good idea to reinvest in stocks as soon as a graph shows a decline. It might be the case that it will shoot back up right away. The investor does need to display some patients.

BUYING AND SELLING WHILE LOOKING AT CHARTS

For those who are visual learners, stock charts changes may mean something on a buy-or-sell strategy. Charts are not representative of when it is important to buy or actually sell a stock but is an analysis of what the buyers and sellers of that stock are doing. In addition, it is either a price trend or reversal mentioned earlier in this chapter. Sometimes there is what is called an "extension" of a price. This is when everything is just sort of stagnant and remains the same. This does not mean it does not increase or decrease, but it tends to stay among the same numbers. If they are not already there, you can visualize a pair of parallel lines, which will just about cover these movements on the exterior within the perimeters. A lot of times investors panic and sell when what was once viewed as a normal pattern for the stuck suddenly goes out of these so called perimeters. In contrast, resistance is when the stock goes up while support is when the stock goes down. It seems it would be the other way around, but it is not. To get even more technical, some investors may view declining volume as an opportunity to drive prices up while those get-rich-quick investors may see a disappearing trend as the end of a positive thing. No investor thinks the same.

SELL SHORT OR STAY IN

Charts are great in that they show when a price is peaking. This is selling-short. Short-sellers make money in a downward trend. This is when you buy shares from a broker (borrower) and then pay them back later. The difference then between the sell price, the buy price, and the broker's commission is what you gain. But should you decide to buy these stocks back, and then you would lose money, if the shares were rising. When online, this is considered a "margin" or short" account, and once you execute your purchase, this is then called a short position. Interestingly enough, when dividends are paid out, they are actually paid to the broker. The goal is to return the number of shares you have borrowed from the margin account at a "lower" price. Otherwise, there is no profit.

WEB SITES

www.futuresource.com

www.prophetfinance.com

www.tfc-charts.w2d.com

www.prophet finance.com

Charts have technical indicators, which keep up with the price of a stock and its moving averages, the volume and momentum. Any change in the average share price in a chart is recorded over a specific time frame. By tracking this via a chart, investors can make an assumption on a "likely" future direction. These movements can be observed best when there are fast movements with little price exchange. Indicators are very standard among most charts and software programs. Closing prices over a certain number of days divided by the result of the number of those prices equal a moving average. Once a moving average shows a trend, which is either below or above its actual line, then assumptions can be made representing a time to buy or sell a stock. What is known as a moving average convergence divergence is another indicator, which stays permanent in the market as a solid line on a chart. Most times this MACD line representing a closing price. Meanwhile a line that is plotted is a dotted line, which would mean it is slower. The plan is to observe whether or not this line crosses the "signal line." If so, this would mean an investor would need to take a short or long strategy. All of this is represented on a chart histogram. The volume of a stock is another indicator that looks out for price and volume changes excluding those stocks that are bought and sold. And then momentum looks at the rate of a change while observing the direction of share price. Additionally, there is a Relative Strength Index. These portray the rate of change in the price of a share.

INDICATORS	
MACD line	solid
Slower movement line	dotted
Signal lines	Move above or below
Below to Above Signal Line	Long position strategy
Above to Below Signal Line	Short position strategy
SAR	Stop and Reverse Points; Dotted lines that represent a trend
Parabola	A fast upward move
Volume	Price and volume Trends
Momentum	Rate of change and direction
RSI	Rate of change in the price of a share

INDICATORS	
Stochastic	A representation of when a market is overbought or oversold
Wave Charts	Long stock or market cycle observations

CHART PATTERNS

Technical analysis also includes those patterns represented in each chart. There are continuation and reversal pattern in charts. As indicated, a continuation pattern is when a share price continues in the same direction. This includes any direction from the actual starting point in which a trend can be observed. In contrast, a reversal pattern simply means that continuation is in a changing mode. With continuation patters there are different forms including flags, gaps, triangles, pennants, rectangles and wedges. When there is a strong trend in a chart a flag-like shape will appear representing some sort of a continuation. It means there is a small price range based on the decreasing volume of a stock. If there is a declining trend, the flag looks as if it is upwards; vice versa if there is an upward trend. And just as the title indicates, a gap in a chart means there is a period of time where there is a break in a price movement. Keep in mind this is not always considered a continuation and may be a reversal. Gaps can represent price breaks that are out of range in conjunction with a price reversal (breakaway), those gaps that are rare (runaways) indicate a continued trend while an exhaustion gap happens in a fast-paced observation of share prices. This may also be a reversal pattern. A weak trend is an exhaustion gap.

Pennants look like the candlestick patterns. They are straight lines representing the highs and the lows meaning volume is declining since the share price goes up or down quickly in a short amount of time. They look like the scary pumpkin teeth carved during Halloween. A rectangle forms when there is a breakout among a price swing where the resistance line and support line are both reached in a pattern. A rectangle can literally be drawn around this pattern. Also, a triangle looks like a triangle of any shape, which represents resistance. Just as a rectangle can be drawn perfectly around a pattern, so can a triangle. As a price breaks out in the same direction it will continue but if it is opposite then it is a reversal. A wedge also shows boundaries, which are slanted to an apex, as does the triangle. Slants against a trend represent a continuation. A following of a trend means there is a reversal.

As an example of a reversal, there may be two peaks that are attached. Both are exactly the same height and both have exactly the same bottoms. When two lines can be drawn straight across the top or bottom, this represents a reversal. In a double top or bottom situation, share prices tend to rise and fall return back to the original peaks or close to it. It then reverses. A head and shoulders reversal pattern is the most common although it looks more like the head and shoulders of a ghost that dresses up on Halloween with the white sheet. This pattern shows a share price when it moves up or reverts forming one shoulder, followed by another dip and then an increase rising to the highest peak. This pattern is known as a "bullish reversal sign anticipating the end of a bear market. It may also be called a reverse head-and-shoulders pattern. A saucer top or bottom pattern looks like an upside down cup. This pattern leaved a trend in which the share price is rising, but then turns slowly into a reversal. An investor should learn to predict breakouts.

Line Charts — Used for observation in long-term trends among a stock option. Like algebra, the price sits on the Y-axis while the time is on the X-axis. These charts are easy to read, as trend changes are easier to spot. Volatility makes the lines move, providing new information on a regular basis.

Bar Charts — A little more detailed than a line chart but similar in nature with periods. A bar exists, and the top represents a high point while the bottom means the low-point. To the left of that bar is the opening price while to the right is the closing. These charts show patterns in which mathematical formulas forecast changes in the charts. Changes are viewed by supply and demand via the indicators.

Candlesticks — On this chart, a vertical line will extend from a high to low point of a share price. The base of the vertical line is round while a horizontal line will represent a stock's opening price and the next line would be a stock's closing price. The symbols will look like random candle sticks on a chart with different shapes and sizes. If the body of the "candle" is white it means the price during the closing period was higher than it was at opening. Meanwhile a black candle represents the price was lower. The main purpose of this chart is to analyze share price movements over a shorter time frame.

CASE STUDY: STEPHEN BIGALOW

Owner

Candlestick Forum LLC

39 W Trace Creek Dr.

The Woodlands, TX 77381

www.candlestickforum.com

(281) 465-9843 - direct

(866) 251-4015

If the investor wants to get specific on a certain type of investing or chart, the Candlestick Forum is the place for those interesting in day trading, futures and commodities trading, or the general psychology of reading candlestick charts. The Candlestick Forum sight has been readily available since 2001. Stephen Bigalow, owner of Candlestick, offers training courses, chatrooms, and more, all focused on this niche. "The main purpose of the site is to provide constant training without a broker." Bigalow himself became an investor 30-years-ago and 20-years-ago is when the candlestick expertise all began. Claiming to be one of the tope three most knowledgeable individuals on the subject matter, Bigalow welcomes all investors with questions on the Web site. With regards to a first-time investor, "I tell people they are often mislead by Wall Street in that they are not taught to invest by the gurus, but are kept at arms length while satisfying the investor enough in that they will continue to go back." Bigalow explains in detail how to make observations of the technical indicators in addition to trends and signals. In a candlestick observation, a stock is represented as in an oversold condition and the probability is extremely high that a new uptrend will start.

Meanwhile, if an overbought condition exists, a downtrend should be expected based on these candlestick signals; further explained in detail. The Japanese rice traders began this trend with at least 60 signals provided over the last 400 years. Bigalow explains there are 12 that work most effectively for investors'. There are 40 reversal and trading signal patterns "Prices don't move based upon fundamentals, but rather the perception of fundamentals," Bigalow said. Training classes are offered for members in

CASE STUDY: STEPHEN BIGALOW

addition to chat rooms. Memberships that stay strong are those that build up communities in such a way compared to an investment club. Daily, up to three stock picks are made by Bigalow which assist investor in making confident decisions about choices. Bigalow is the author of Profitable Candlestick Trading and High Profit Candlesticks. "As long as there is investor sediment, these signals work well," Bigalow said.

Why should you become a Member of the Candlestick Trading Forum?

- You will be exposed to the best stock trade candlestick signals for the day.

- You will be provided with the best-researched commodity and futures trades available through candlestick analysis.

- You will learn why the trades were recommended, using new candlestick investing concepts.

- You will learn to detect the investment sentiment behind each signal, providing powerful insights into future price movement.

- You will be joining an ever-growing group of like-minded candlestick trading experts, each contributing their individual knowledge and research to the Candlestick Trading Forum.

Tickers — These charts are formulated when a specific number of trades take place. These are similar to the candle charts, although they are used for observation of momentum. If trading is fast it is salient as the candles moves really fast. When the period is slow, there is no momentum to speak of. Most investors observe this chart when stocks are trading over a million shares on a daily basis, promising a lot of activity. This is for the "scalpers" who make trades within minutes or even seconds.

Point-and-figure chart — This chart is purely for trends. Like the line charts, the Y-axis represents price while the X is time. When there is a positive trend and things are looking up, an X will be marked. An O would mean negative or a downward reversal.

TECHNICAL AND FUNDAMENTAL ANALYSIS WITH CHARTS

In choosing your stock, there is fundamental analysis and technical analysis. Generally speaking, private and institutional investors in deciding on a purchase use the fundamental analysis. On the technical side, short-term traders generally use this. The financial stability of a company coupled with economic supply and demand is used with fundamental analysis. The P/E ratios, annual growth rate, and earnings records of the stock are looked at in this type of analysis. Most investors using this type of analysis are not overly concerned with the ups and downs of the stock market; rather they want a stock with steady growth in which their investments will continue to prosper until the time comes to sell. There are commodities, brokers, and traders that rely on fundamentals such as the weather. Other economical factors involved include shortages of certain products, whether it is gasoline or gold. Since the research in this analysis takes a fair amount of time, the short-term traders tend not to use this. Technical analysis is a study of sentiment, time, and price. This is typically done by using a chart. This quickly shows the history of a stock's price minus the lengthy research that could be involved. Most short-term traders really pay attention to the increases and decreases to fit the mold of a certain purchase.

With technical analysis, the most successful use is to move money when the risk is the lowest. Technical analysts consider the following four things: 1) Examining long market or stock cycles, which is called a wave theory; 2) Examining stock price movement with no time factor, this is called a point-dash-and-dash figure theory; 3) Examining each trading period for the relationships between the prices, which is called the candle stick theory; 4) Using mathematical formulas is called bar-chart theory. Most technical analysts feel that the average daily volume of trading is very important. There are four phases to a stock trend's life cycle, in which volume is very important. This is accumulation; institutional investors buy small quantities at a time. Mark-up represents a rise in price on a daily basis with higher volume. Third, distribution occurs when a stock stays idle, meaning it does not increase or decrease much. This would be a time to be concerned with the outcome of a stock because there would really be no point in staying. Markdowns show a downward trend little by little and then start to plummet with high volume. Volume activity is attributed to large institution involvement such as pensions, hedge funds, trusts, and banks.

The main things to keep in mind when observing charts are time frames, objectives, price performances, growth, history, price indicators, and moving averages. Settings can be changed in some instances.

BENCHMARKS

Benchmarking is also another good reason to keep a chart. They are used to evaluate the performance of a stock while comparing the performance of other stocks. Many of the software programs use a benchmark, but every company has a set benchmark as a reached (or un-reached) goal. If the stock is not reaching that peak then new scenarios can be created. It can be looked at as a tool, referencing measurement. Another way to look at the benchmarks is "ways in which investors can set a challenge and reach it." With investment portfolios, benchmarking is primarily used to make comparisons among indexes such as the Russell 2000, NASDAQ Composite, and S&P 500. With charts, comparisons do not have to be observed every day but in enough time, on a monthly basis. If the investor's goal is not being reached, then it is time to crank up the investment intensity. Think logically and be sure to compare your stocks to others of similar nature. It is just not wise to compare a mouse to an elephant. Many of our domestic pension funds compare the real estate portfolios to the Lehman aggregate. It is viewed at a "broad bond market" index in addition to the S&P 500. Those investors that are more aggressive would vie that of NASDAQ or Russell 2000. Pension funds and sharks usually view these indexes annually, measuring performance. From this, it is observed where shifts can be made in the investment portfolios. Patterns will represent area where poor or positive performances exist. Often, benchmarks are measured annually although three to five years is sufficient to some, because advisors, stocks, and funds can be credited as good for the long-term investors. It is not always a good idea to reinvest in stocks as soon as a graph shows a decline. It might be the case that it will shoot back up right away. The investor does need to display some patience.

WEB SITES

www.bigcharts.com

www.clearstation.com

www.investor.com

www.profitfinance.com

www.stockcharts.com

www.megastock.com

www.omegaresearch.com

www.moneycentral.msn.com/investor

www.wallstreetcity.com

CHAPTER 10

Taxes

Most of us do not feel like messing with taxes, and this applies to stock taxes too. There are two ways in which you can be taxed, that is capital gains tax and dividend income tax. When you sell your stock for a profit, this is a capital gain. This also applies to your homes, machinery, land, et cetera, but in regards to stock you will be taxed on your profit or loss. There are both long-term and short-term gains. If you sell in less than a year's time, this is short-term, and the IRS taxes your profit as a regular income meaning you will be taxed on it at least 25 percent or more. With your ordinary income, this includes wages and interest income. Capital gains are apparent when you sell your stock more than its basis price. Long-term gains are anything over a year; it is 5 percent if you are in a lower tax bracket, but 25 percent if you are in a higher tax bracket. In 2008, this 5 percent capital gain tax will be 0 for people in the two lowest income brackets on sales of stocks, mutual funds and securities set by the Internal Revenue Service code. With dividend taxes you are taxed at 15 percent but there is a tax relief provision in which you could be taxed as a though it is your main source of income as well. Some people drop stock in an attempt to offset both gains and losses with less tax. The IRS does have what is called a wash rule in which the investor is not allowed to sell stock and then turn around quickly to buy it back in an attempt to avoid capital loss. These current tax rates are set to expire in 2008, so it is wise to follow up with a tax assistant. Your company will send you a letter on what you lost, dividends, what you owe on taxes, and more.

With a short-term loss where there is no long-term activity, each year you can deduct up to $3,000 of that loss against your ordinary income. If the loss exceeds $3,000 the investor can carry the excess loss over to the next year. A carryover to the next year is still considered a short-term loss. If you have no short-term activity but a long-term loss, the deductions are the same. Under short-term activity and long-term loss, the investor can deduct the $3,000 against ordinary income while carrying the excess into the next year then this carryover is considered a long-term loss. Meanwhile, in a net short-term loss and a net long-term loss, again you can deduct your $3,000 of the loss against your regular income. This deduction is then applied against your short-term losses first. Then if you have any unused deduction amount carried into the next year the deduction applies to your short-term loss. A net short-term loss with a net long-term gain; if the gain exceeds the loss, then the gain is considered long-term and is taxed at a favorable rate. If the short-term loss exceeds the long-term gain, your overall loss is considered as short-term. A net short-term gain with net long-term loss is when the gain is larger than the loss and the investor's net gain is considered short-term and taxed at the ordinary income rate. If the loss is more than the gain, it is considered long-term and the investor can deduct up to $3,000 against the main income while any access can be carried over again. If you have to take a capital loss, the best time is to take it in a year when you have either no gains or your capital gains are short-term.

CDS

If you are considering a certificate of deposit, the accounts are fixed for a set term. They pay higher interest rates than other options and should an investor decide to pull out of the term, there is a penalty. When speaking of a penalty, this includes forfeiture of interest as well as principal. Losing part of the principal however, is not always the case. This penalty is tax-deductible. At times in our lives things come up and we need to shift money from one account to another. It is best to avoid this, but in any instance, funds that were currently being received from the account, are funds that get the deductions. Usually, the principal is not affected in this instance unless the penalty is large enough to eat up an interest payment and that interest is still then not paid off. In any time deposit account, it is a standard regulation where certain conditions have to be met. This includes that actual maturity date. Pulling out before that maturity date could automatically mean a loss. When there are savings certificates involved, a forfeiture of an initial discount will also cause a penalty on any early withdrawal. This usually involves those with fixed maturities of more than one year. If an investors daughter or son, for example, is going to college within the next five years, it would be wise to set that maturity date for the five years or four perhaps in which case when the time comes there will be no penalties. Another alternative to this is putting a few thousand here, and a few thousand there; just in case. No one ever complains about having more than one account. There are what is called a 12-month CD. In this case, you only have to be good for a year with the money, and then that CD could be reinvested elsewhere into an account were a higher interest rate may exist. Our favorite part of the year, tax time, forfeited amounts will arrive to both the IRS and the investor on a 1099 form in which case, deductions can be made on a 1040 form.

Bankrate.com
www.bankrate.com

BankQuote
www.banxquote.com

iMoney.net
imoneynet.com

STOCK INVESTMENT LOSSES AND TAXES

Capital loss is the difference between what is received from a sale and what was paid for it to begin with.

Let's pretend that after reading this book you will begin

making really good investment moves and the portfolio starts getting "fat." Fat is good. At sometime, certain assets are bound to be a loss. These losses could be tax deductible. All "capital losses," are deductible in full, offsetting capital gains for that specific year. When a loss exceeds a gain, $3,000 could offset that gain which would be a salary and interest income. Remember that: if capital losses are more than $3,000, any excess amount, can rollover into the next year. Capital losses are normal as people are selling the stocks all the time or any other asset. To make a long story short, if you put in $8,000, and sell those assets for $6000, you still have $2,000. Because the actual capital loss was $2000, there is nothing that could be forwarded to the next year. Nothing can be deducted unless there is a sell or disposition, which is the same thing because you are ridding of something. In all cases, this information is in regards to those assets where capital is involved, no object that is personal, such as a pinto. An important thing to remember is that reinvested stock dividends, broker commissions, and buying or selling costs are all considered loss additions meaning overall, the actual loss could increase from these items. This is something that people can easily overlook as it is just not something that is thought about.

Guess what, there is a tax law for unfavorable securities. If an investment is made into a company that goes under (bankrupt), that stock investment may be deducted. The law is on your side, because when things like this happen, people can lose it all. A decision is made based on whether a stock loss is short or long-term. A short-term loss is that which is loss in less than a year whereas a long-term loss is when a security is held for more than a year. This is an ordinary capital loss which could be up to $50,000 or

$100,000 on a joint return. If the stock had value in the precedent year and then the stock becomes exceptionally "worthless," then it can be written-off in the taxes. This can be checked via year-end statements. In any case where a stock company resists doing more business, goes bankrupt, or becomes insolvent, these facts must be proven to claim an actual loss. Again, these losses are made on the IRS Form 1040.

ANOTHER RULE FROM THE INTERNAL REVENUE CODE — DECTION 1244 STOCK

The IRS says if an investor has 1244 stock, these investments should be treated as an "ordinary loss" and not a capital loss. This type of stock includes those corporations, preferred or common where equity is not greater than $1 million when that stock was issued. Other traits are that the investor is the original owner of a stock and the stock had had to be issued as money or property. This could be an inheritance. When we mean ordinary, we mean only $50,000 can be deducted and in a joint return (boyfriend and girlfriend), $100,000 is the limit. Seven years is the time frame where a loss like this can be claimed. The year a security becomes useless, a claim should be made. If it is not "discovered" at that time, then it may be claimed from the date of a return. The law says seven years is enough, anything beyond would mean a bye-bye loss that may never be claimed. All tax losses are limited to the original basis, meaning what you originally paid for is what brings the benefit. My guess is that most investors would figure out within seven years that their stock was not worth a dime, but, things happen.

TAX DEDUCTIONS FROM NEWSLETTERS AND ONLINE SERVICES

Deductions can be made under the "miscellaneous" category when subscriptions are made to online services, including newsletters or investment newspapers. This is special for those "investors" only. If an online service is used with investments, deductions may be made. If a service is personal, then that person would not qualify. If it is a mixed situation, then deduction related to the investments should be made and then the investor would qualify. Another advantage to this is that all or half may be claimed and the rest can be claimed the following year. All of the above deductions are geared for a Form 1040 only. Not a 1040A, 1040 X or whatever other letters may be involved.

TAXES ON BROKER COMMISSION AND FEES

Commission to a broker may not be deducted, but a fee to an investment advisor can be. This can be confusing because an investment advisor may have a fee and commission. One is one and the other is the other. Keep in mind that commissions for a broker are always added to the cost basis. Fees can be added to the miscellaneous category on a 1040. Should an advisor charge for both a fee and a commission, on one occasion, just separate that fee from the commission and deduct it. The characteristics of a fee are either flat-fees or hourly rates. These advisors to not make profits off of any investments that are made. They are strictly there to help with a plan.

BONDS HAVE TAX BENEFITS, TOO

In a savings bond, all interest on E bonds and I bonds can be deferred. This can be done with any time frame until that bond has reached its maturity date. Nothing has to be done about this on an annual basis when tax season comes around. If an investor wishes, interest on a savings bond does not have to be deferred. Interest could be taxed at a lower rate, which could benefit some depending on the income situation. With a Series EE bonds, interest rates are "fixed" until maturity or redemption. With a Series I bond, these interest rates are not fixed and are adjusted on a semiannual basis, according to inflation.

Bond premium= A bond purchased at a price greater than its face value. The premium is the excess.

Corporate bonds are considered taxable. With a bond premium, it is amortized beginning the year it was purchased. For all years an investor owns a bond, taxable interest can be offset due to an amortizable premium amount. If a bond is purchased for $6000 when it was worth $5,500, that extra $500 is what gets amortized. That money divided by the years equals $100, which can offset the actual interest due on the bond. Municipal bonds on the other hand are tax exempt. Any premium with a municipal bond has to be amortized. People should choose to amortize the premium because if you do not, then there may be a capital loss during the final redemption period. This is not necessary with an IRA or retirement plan because interest is not deductible anyway.

C CORPORATION STOCKS AND SMALL BUSINESS DEDUCTIONS

Investing in small businesses can be beneficial when it comes to taxes. It also supports the smaller business, which in hope would turn out to be a profitable decision. Small businesses are considered C Corporations stocks in existence since 1993. Assets of small business should be up top the $50 million range, gross. The business cannot be an investment company and should be active. This would mean that at least 80 percent of the business is "qualified."

A QUALIFIED BUSINESS EXCLUDES

Architecture

Brokerage Services

Banking

Performing Arts

Law Practice

Hotel Management

Farming

Insurance

Actuarial Science

Engineering

Health

Financial Services

And anything similar.

Stock that is inherited or gifted does not fit the mold for a small business stock. The plus side of this stock is that there is rollover benefits where as a stock must be held for six months or more before being disposed. A 50-percent exclusion is allowable if the stock has been in existence for five years.

Note: Deferred gain must be done within 60 days.

EXAMPLE

If a stock is sold and $15,000 is gained and a new stock is purchased for $30,000, then only $15,000 is owed because of the earlier $15,000 deferred gain. If that stock increased to $50,000 and is sold, then taxable gain would be $35,000 as long as there is no other involvement where a deferral or exclusion was involved. This would be nice for two-month time period.

FOREIGN TAXES

For those investments made in foreign countries in either stocks or mutual funds, write-offs can be made. Investors can deduct the taxes as an itemized deduction on the 1040 or may claim a "tax credit." For some reason, those taxes must be in similarity to that of the U.S. tax. It is law that those countries engaging in terrorist activities cannot be used as a tax write-off, stated by the Internal Revenue Service. Of the two choices, "claiming the credit" would be the best option because tax liability is actually reduced. Claiming either a deduction or a credit in this instance is done with a 1099-DIV Form.

INVESTMENT COMPUTERS DEDUCTIBLE!

In any case where a home computer is used for investment activities, certain things may be deductible. The number one rule is that the computer must be purely for investment activities and not for personal use too. But again, if used of personal and investment, the investment portion use can be subtracted. This can be entered as a miscellaneous deduction in Form 1040. Even if the computer is being leased it can be deducted. The cost of a computer can be deducted as well, but the entire cost may not be included as a write off.

RETIREMENT ACCOUNTS & TAXES

The law encourages investors to work more toward retirement account. The plus is that some contributions and savings can be written-off. Since IRAs serve many as retirement funds, the government assists in that tax deductions can take place under certain circumstances. The government is helping you save money through these deductions. While the government does not assist with all of your contribution when it comes to taxes, it may help with 1/3 of 3/3, depending on what the tax bracket is really. As mentioned earlier in this book, the contribution limit is $4,000 or $5,000 if the saver is over 50. A spouse may only contribute twice as much when he/she is saving for both of them and can afford it. All tax is deferred and withdrawals have to be made after the age of 70 ½.

With a 401K plan, tax deductions can be made with contributions and is adjusted accordingly in the "gross income" section.

When making contributions to an IRA, a person may not use unemployment compensation, investment income including dividends and interest, foreign income, or deferred compensation with pensions and annuities. And deductions can't be made if there is any involvement in any other retirement plan.

Note: If a man is 70 ½ years old, he can no longer contribute to an IRA however he can contribute to that IRA on behalf of his 60-year-old wife.

MODIFIED ADJUSTED GROSS INCOME

With an IRA, a MAGI plays a role in contribution deductions. It cannot exceed a "phase-out" range. MAGI is referred to as adjusted gross income. It is based upon exclusions for interest with the IRA in the Unites States saving bonds. These particular bonds are geared for foreign earned income, higher education and adjusted gross income. In 2007, for example, a phase-out is in the range of $83,000 to $103,000 if married and filing jointly for an IRA and for those who are single, would have been somewhere in the range of $52,000 to $62,000.

YOUR MONEY AND IRAS

While contributing to an IRA, an investor may purchase stocks, bonds, mutual funds, CDs or any other investment vehicle. Certain vehicle that is not permitted under an IRA charge a penalty fee. If under the age of 59 1/2, that fee could be up to 10. In other matters, an investor may not be penalized for an early distribution penalty if the IRS has placed levies on your IRA for back taxes, you are unemployed and receiving unemployment benefits for twelve consecutive weeks, money is used to pay medical expenses (exceeds 7.5 percent of your income), the money is used to pay higher education expenses, or someone becomes disabled. A penalty may also take place if a person passes and the heirs withdraw the money.

Note: Foreign investments are allowable, but foreign taxes paid from an IRA cannot be credited or deducted.

EXCESS TAX

Should the IRS increase the MAGI above your phase-out range and you cannot claim an IRA deduction due to your income, people are subject to an excess tax. Because an IRA deduction cannot be reported on a return, this tax is up to 6 percent. Each year on, the tax will be applied to earnings on contributions made to that IRA. This excess can be applied to another year if requested. This means if one year you were able to deduct so much money from your IRA and another year were not able to due to the MAGI increase, that precedent year can be designated which would make the 6 percent penalty. In any case where one year an investor was not eligible for the deductions, that year can be used to counteract the 6 percent penalty. Refer to the IRS codes for more information.

The Roth IRA is our newest option, just a few years old. The difference between a traditional IRA and a Roth is that there is no immediate tax break as contributions are not deductible. The Roth offers a long-term tax savings. People can withdraw from this fund without a penalty, at any time, tax-free. Another benefit that people use is the conversion of the traditional IRA to a Roth IRA (mentioned earlier). Investors due have to pay income tax on the account, but if the account (Roth) is open for five years, then there may be no penalty on early distribution if under the age of 59 ½. The catch to this is that a person's income must be less than $100,000 and again, if there is a spouse, items have to be filed jointly. The account is built up on a tax-free basis.

TAX-FREE CONVERSIONS

In an IRA rollover, investors can transfers funds from one account to another with no tax consequences on certain conditions. Avoiding current tax, direct transfers from one IRA to another will avoid taxes and withdrawing funds from an IRA and then replacing them within 60 days also avoids current taxes. Whatever the situation, this includes account from brokerage to brokerage or from one IRA to a mutual fund. The IRS does not mess around. Should the taxpayer decide to withdraw money with the intention of return it within that 60-day time period, if the return is one day late, the entire account will be taxed.

401(K) NOTE

With a company's 401(k), the amount the employee contributes to a plan and the actual amount left over in the salary should be reported. The actual amount earned after contributing to the IRA is what needs to be on the tax return. This is an elective deferral or salary reduction and the amount left after the contribution is what is taxed. The law does set a maximum amount on the elective deferral limits. When starting a job the employer should explain these options more in detail and can assist with an elective deferral plan. Companies have eligibility requirements for these plans. Not all employers are good at explaining these things so it is wise to seek the help of a tax professional at a sooner position, and not a latter.

DIVIDENDS AND TAXES

There is no tax break from the IRS when dividends are involved. Each year all dividends should be taxed as ordinary income. Taxes owed are based on an individual's tax bracket. The more money someone makes, the more taxes that have to be paid. If you are in a 30 percent bracket and the dividend is $1000, for example, then federal tax would be based on $300.

Internal Revenue Service
www.irs.gov

National Association of Enrolled Agents
www.nara.org

◀ CHAPTER 11 ▶

Random Thoughts

This chapter is about people and their stories and those investors that are seemingly "advanced." An advanced investor is one who can get by just fine without a broker and be successful. Often times investors amateur or not are lacking in confidence when it comes to making investment decisions on their own. This is why most turn to brokers. But once you become comfortable and content with your current investments, you become advanced in that particular area. A broker is no longer needed at this point if the right research is done. Zeroing in on a particular company, its financial status, rates of returns, and ratios represents the point when the investor is somewhat advanced as these key concepts really represent what the stock itself is all about. Keep up with the economy and a specific investments industry gives the investor a distinct advantage over failing investments without having to pay fees. In this aspect, the company performance should be reviewed for at least the three precedent years. Of course stock quotes are always representative of a company, but history does tend to repeat itself. Even if it does not, it is always important to know what a stock's pattern is. Meanwhile, observing demand for a company product should also be taken into consideration while comparing to like-kind or competition companies within the same industry. Wall Street provides what is called an analysts evaluation, which goes as far as digging into the backgrounds of corporate officers within a noted stock company.

In observing a company's reputation along with its products, you can guesstimate on the success of that product and compare it to past situation where another product within that same company was introduced to the market. The question is how do these products perform. From this a sudden increase or decrease in a company is lucrative or not with its investment decisions. Using Coca-Cola as an example, soft drinks products are constantly coming out with new products with additional flavors to either outdo or keep up with the competition. These changes can adversely affect the way a stock can perform so the investor should expect these possibilities by keeping up with press releases or what have you, and staying informed on the latest changes. This is obviously a company that has gained the respect of the world not to mention a reputation leaving some comfort to an investor who knows the product has been around for a while. It sounds like a lot of work, but if you just consider that it's one company, it's really not that much work.

A company background is the key also in determining a successful stock on your own. These options are made available via Web sites including:

WEB SITES	
CorpWatch	www.corpwatch.org
CorporateInformation.com	www.corporateinformation.com
Corptech	www.corptech.com
U.S. Business Reporter	www.activemedia-guide.com
Hoover's Online	www.hoovers.com

In viewing economic activity, investors can get all the details through Web sites where extremely detailed information can be found including inventory moves, quarterly information, monthly reports, sales information, research and so forth depending on what company it is you are looking into.

WEB SITES	
Bitpipe	www.bitpipe.com
Bloomberg National and World Indices	www.bloomberg.com/markets/ stocks/mover_index_ibov.html
Bureau of Economic Analysis	www.bea.doc.gov/bea/dn/home/ gdp.htm
CBS MarketWatch.com	cbs.marketwatch.com
CBS Market Watch Industry Alerts	www.marketwatch.com
Chicago Fed National Activity Index	www.chicagofed.org/economic_ research_and_data/cfnai.cfm
DataMonitor	www.datamonitor.com
Durable Goods Orders	www.census.gov/indicator/www/ m3

WEBSITES	
Economic Cycle Research Institute	www.businesscycle.com/data.php
Economic-Indicators.com	www.economic-indicators.com
Existing Home Sales	www.realtor.org
Federal Reserve Statistical Release, Industrial Production and Capacity Utilization	www.federalreserve.gov/releases/g17
Fuld & Company	www.fuld.com/i3/index.html
Leading Economic Indicators	www.conference-board.org/economics/indicators.cfm
Manufacturing and Trade Inventories and Sales	www.census.gov/mtis/www/mtis.html
New Home Sales from the National Association of Home Builders	www.nahb.org
Producer Price Indexes	www.bls.gov/ppi/home.htm
STAT-USA	www.stat-usa.gov
The Beige Book, Current Economic Conditions	www.federalreserve.govfomc/beigebook/2004
U.S. Census Bureau Construction Spending	www.census.gov/ftp/pub/const/www/c30index.html
Yahoo Industry News	biz.yahoo.com/industry

REALITY ON THE AVERAGE PEOPLE

Thoughts from random people

YOUNG INVESTORS

Most of the generation in the 20 – 30-year-old age group is not that familiar with the different types of investing. Part of it is that school systems do not cover this topic and then it might be the case that parents themselves do not know much about investing, let alone their children. The biggest investment that the average person makes is the purchase of a home. People often get stuck in a rut and get used to a certain way of doing things. The reality is (as state earlier in the book) that a good investor should start young. With the governmental and presidency issues these days, who knows what the future will entail 50 years from now. Many references have been cited in this book, including Web sites for the adult investor to get started, leaving plenty of work to do. There are Web sites available for children in which they can learn to invest at a very young age. Not using your money of course, but it teaches them the purpose and reasoning behind investing, making it easier as they get older. A.G. Edwards (now merging to Wachovia) offered *Big Money Adventure*, a site where children as young as two can get online and play games that involve stock-picking. Another Web site is The Young Investor Web site communities are available for both the children and parents as well, offering the basics of investing. For those parents who are ahead of the game, you are super.

COLLEGE-AGED INVESTORS

A lot of the time, college-aged individuals do not have much money. Many have to borrow school loans, and barely make ends meet trying to work while going to school fulltime. Money is always an issue, as it seems to be scarce, especially to those whose parents are not supporting them. Some sites that are beneficial to this type of investor include Edustock (**library.thinkquest.org/3088**) and Independent Means (**www.anincomeofherown.com**). Independent means caters to women while Edustock is really meant for all ages for beginners. Most of the time and individual's situation varies and options are not made available to them. Often times, employers will not encourage individuals or make them aware that investing elsewhere could be beneficial in the future.

STEPHANIE HICKS IN TEXAS DISCUSSES STOCKS IN AN EMAIL. STEPHANIE IS 26-YEARS-OLD AND IS A REALTOR:

"It's a good thing that you are writing a book because I think that a lot of people from our generation don't understand investing (well at least around here). I know I didn't know near as much as I learned while in college."

FROM LACEY GATLIN, A 27-YEAR-OLD NURSE, IN FLORIDA:

"Umm let's see, Tony who works for UPS has a better retirement plan than me. He has stock and great stock options, I do not. He has a 401(k), I have a 403b since I work at a hospital and it is a nonprofit organization. I don't know what a REIT is. And the only investment strategies that I know of are age appropriate, as far as some one who is in their 50s would probably invest more conservatively than I would. So that's all I know, not very much, I'll leave that up to Tony."

In hearing from the above two people and a few others, it is true that the younger generation that should be investing is not real fond of the subject matter, however more knowledge comes with age. Granted, it would also depend on the type of environment a person has been raised in although all environments and different parts of the world are unique, so are individuals.

SENIOR INVESTORS

It may just be my imagination, but it seems that most senior citizens know what they are doing by the time they retire when it comes to investing. Many own several homes, RVs, with CDs, mutual funds and are obviously set for retirement because they do things right in preparing for the future.

In contrast, Lee Ruggels, a retiree from Kansas has made observation that a lot of older folks are "dreadfully unhappy as their entire investment income is from money markets tied to directly to prime interest rates. And a big cut in the prime by the Federal Reserve puts a big cut in those individuals' food supply." Meanwhile, "being an ultra-safe retired investor is not safe, it is quite dangerous for the relatively healthy," Ruggels said. A retired senior, Ruggels and his wife live comfortably traveling back and forth from their antiquated Kansas home to California where their children live, because they can. Ruggels explains that no matter what age you are, the investor should always look at an investment horizon as 10 to 20-years and not 10 to 20 months. I asked Ruggels how much he knew when he was in his 20s, the answer being "I knew nothing." He began on his own in his 20s when he invested in a life insurance policy that had a small, but seemingly increasing value. It turned out to be a bad investment and a bad idea he has avoided since then.

As most do these days people look to their careers and invest in 401Ks. The same idea existed with Ruggels long-term career when he began investing with TIAA-CREF. The company contributed a certain amount of money which he matched. His employer offered no advice on what to do for future planning, Ruggels said he "did what most did, split 50-50 between stocks and bonds; another bad mistake. By the age of 30, Ruggels almost gave up and didn't do much research, but he stuck with the stocks. Eventually his company came up with a program called "Consumer Financial Decisions," in which he could assist with actual surveys, having to do with investment matters. The focus was a cross-section of adults where national interviews were conducted on investment issues and how much people knew about it. The survey was geared for families of all age groups.

Things have worked out for the family though. Ruggels's mother had a surprising amount of savings, which had been kept in CDs. He took over her finances when she began aging, doing more research. At this point, he allocated to funds in what he thought were well-rated companies such as Vanguard and Fidelity. At this point, it wasn't TIAA-CREF that was holding his money. Ruggels said using the financial publications such as Smart Money and miscellaneous other items. He learned the importance of looking up the company portfolios. Other proceeds from elsewhere inheritance where allocated to mutual funds. This also includes real estate sales. These funds are said to be "heavy into the stocks." But his overall goal was planning for retirement when he did invest quite a bit into retirement funds.

The greatest advice Ruggels could share is to "never use insurance, start out early with almost everything, and diversify in stocks. Those advanced investors and fans tend to do as they please, but as a serious investor, you should use targeted funds, which bring more assurance to your future. As a solo decision making investor other advice is to pay attention without running away every time there is a recession.

MORE WORDS FROM THE WISE...

ON INDIVIDUAL INVESTMENTS

Mrs. Ruggels final job began to offer an annuity on a matched payment basis, in which they matched what she contributed. She participated for five years before terminating the plan. This began about 1990. Her own total investment was about $5,000. During the years she had to wait until the money reached its payout date, the investment company went broke. Despite that, her payout was $20,000.

Mrs. Ruggels recalls when the US government began to offer a tax benefit on somewhere in the range of $3,000 if it was invested in an IRA. At this point, she sought the advice of a broker and took his advice on stocks. On the whole she made money each year - $2,000 or better per year. This too was about 1990. Beginning to manage her own money about 2000, she used various information sources. Value line Investment Guide, Money Magazine. Semi regularly various TV business programs for current information about companies were viewed with their production, investigations, scandals, buyouts and so forth. **By the end of 2007 Suzie had made about 150-percent increase on her original investments.** Now annually I review my portfolio, sell the ones I have been disappointed in and invest that money in what I hope will do better."

LEARNING ABOUT INVESTMENTS...

Mrs. Ruggels began to learn about investments in the 1980s when her father would discuss his investments. He died in 1990 and she was my mother's business executor. Her mother had no knowledge or interest in finance and the father had charged her with looking after her. His investments were sound and earned her mother's money so she was not in need at all. In fact, all dividends were ploughed back into the stocks from which they came. The only real change Mrs. Ruggels made was to sell the stock that he had bought on margins and to consolidate her holdings under one broker for her own convenience. That portfolio was a mixture of government investments (Freddy Mac), large companies and a few more risky stocks (e.g. mining). The risky stocks did not pay off.

WHAT ADVICE CAN YOU SHARE FOR THE INVESTORS?

The hardest thing to understand is the complete irrationality of the market. " I never wanted to be a day trader of get rich quick, so my investments were conservative," Mrs. Ruggels said. She noted the importance of getting information about the market and companies on a regular basis and to do research. She invested for a while in Merck and increased her stake in that company stock about 50 percent. When patents on some of their most commercially successful drugs were about to expire she sold out. Not only did the patents expire, but also the FDA began to investigate some of their claims about the effectiveness of the drugs. Stocks Mrs. Ruggels had bought for say $64 a share went to the $90s. She then sold and subsequently they went to $32. By the same token, Mrs. Ruggels bought Jet Blue Airline stock, they had a bad three days during a storm, got tons of bad publicity and their stock has almost disappeared from the scene, so you have to be lucky as well as diligent.

"It is good to diversify your holdings so if tech stocks go down, perhaps alternative energy goes up," Mrs. Ruggels said.

WHEN ASKING ABOUT THE AVERAGE YOUNG INVESTOR...

"It is hard for young persons to get started because they usually have too many expenses on meager starting out salaries to set aside money for a portfolio and to much to do what with beginning a career, perhaps starting a family, buying a house to set aside time to start studying. But stocks come in all price ranges and no-one has to start out with Berkshire Hathaway."

Should a hard-core investor spill coffee all over their laptop, other alternatives are typically available to make trades happen. A lot of times online firms offer trading option over the phone, or even to an actual broker over the phone or via fax. This would be the traditional way of investing, but sometimes you gotta do what you gotta do. This is where the investor needs to pay close attention as commission charges or what have you could suddenly become more expensive. And should a fax have to be made, sending something once is better than sending it twice; you could get charged twice and it does happen. Keep in mind that stocks can be a roller coaster ride soaring and dropping very quickly with no room for mistakes. This is common among high tech stocks and IPOs. Investors are hyped when there are sudden rises or drops in stocks due to exiting and entering, but remember, sometimes it is best to just stay put. And if you have done your research, it is likely, you are in the right place because the investor knows what has been purchased. In my opinion, the risk should be the first question any investor should ask himself or herself. An investor should learn to expect a downfall although it is not necessarily what anyone would want. If you analyze a situation, decisions in the future can be made more carefully. Meanwhile, when executions and confirmations slow down, the reports may be a little slow too. The Internet and technology are both two fast-moving things, and opportunities are going to continue to increase in our future with advancement options. Sometimes an investor needs to be on their toes as the changes as markets change constantly. The Internet will always be viewed as a time saver, but do not forget to include the time for research. Good things will happen for those who do.

WATCH OUT FOR THE MOUSE

Sometimes, if it is not one thing, it is another. Meaning the car broke down and I fixed it, but then I ran out of gas after a tire went flat; all in one day. I hate days like this. What I am getting at is the investor has to be careful when buying online, as sometimes there are problems with brokerage firms that turn out to be a big hassle. If you are not up to speed on DSL or high-speed Internet, I would suggest you "get with the program (Oprah)" because there have been incidents where investors place orders only to find two orders have been placed and not one. And it is all because the computer froze or was too slow meaning that the requested trade did not trade for the price of the stock at that instant and either the investor's cost was too much or not desirable. This would be in an instant of a short-term investment. When the computer is slow and the confirmation does not reach investors, double requests can happen. No one wants to pay twice as much. Little daily events that do not go smoothly can get old after a while.

"No one ever went broke by saying no too often." ~ Harvey Mckay

MY AUNT EDEMNIA

I got in trouble from an elderly aunt named Edemnia after going to the grocery store to pick up a loaf of bread for her. She was so parsimonious that she knew exactly how much that bread cost, with tax. She had seen an ad in the paper for Safeway Stores and that is where I was told to go. So I went and I could not find the bread that had been advertised in the paper for $2 or what have you. If I recall correctly, I even asked one of the workers if they had the bread. I had to find something similar and close to the same price. An extra 20 cents was probably spent and I got in trouble for it. Some people do not mess around when it comes to money. When she passed, I heard she was not doing too badly, financially I mean.

FRUGAL PEOPLE

I grew up in a suburban area in Mesquite, Texas where I could ride my bike on the side walk. I would ride past this man named Ted's house who had three cars and a petite wife who didn't like to drive. He was the father of a friend of the family and the only thing he wore was overalls with holes in them. The holes were patched up with duct tape in any place necessary. He did this for years. My point is, sometimes how people portray themselves on the outside is not what is really happening on the inside. You see, Ted was a pack rack. He saved literally everything. I doubt I will never go in another house that has as much stuff in as this one – ever. When Ted passed he was buried in those overalls because that is what he had wanted. His granddaughter Amy was going through his things one day and she found things stashed everywhere, including money. The man had money stashed in random places throughout the house. He had money stashed in one of the baby shoes of his 50-year-old son. I always liked these people as they were part of my childhood memories and they gave me ice cream.

A TIP ABOUT THE BROKERS

I cannot stress it enough to read the fine lines in any contract. Think about how many times you've signed a contract and you skimmed over everything. Sometimes this can really mess things up and there is nothing you can do about it. The same goes when you choose an online broker. Brokers on and offline include clauses in the contracts stating should any dispute arise, things have to be settled via arbitration. It is the same as real estate contracts but buyers and sellers choose to agree on arbitration, mediation, or both (in the state of California), but with brokers, you don't have a choice. Most people agree to arbitration because it is less costly than a court case and a lawyer. However, lawyers can be involved. There are some other differences involving rights and investigation with arbitration as there would be with a lawsuit, which would require more money and would be more in depth. Claims against brokers can be made via the National Association of Securities Dealers. Arbitration groups do exist in which there is a forum to choose from.

An investor has to prove how money was lost or what have you through proof and documentation in addition to a good explanation. An arbitrator, in the hearing, will simply question both sides. If there is less than $10,000 involved this information is done from both parties through written documents. A decision is based on this. A hearing is necessary when there is more than $10,000 involved but it is less formal. An arbitrator can be an attorney or a retired judge.

YOU DECIDE

In conclusion, the stock market can be viewed in many different ways. It can be an obsession, a hobby, an investment, or part of a political discussion. Whichever way it is viewed, it is a pure reflection of the financial status of the economy. It is affect by interest rates, employment, political events, and inflation among many other things. Because our everyday lives revolve around work, well most of us have to work, and what we call governments, the stock market will continue to be supported and grow strong. It serves everyone for one reason or another helping all of us raise money and expand. It is important that even the individual investors realize the importance of savings. There are some people out there who can barely keep money in the checking accounts. And since the everyday lives are challenging, it is hard for people to save. Therefore, starting small never hurt anything, especially for a long-term investment. I encourage you, the reader to discuss with your friends and family and even the kids, the importance of the future because times are tough when financially, things are not prepared. From the beginning, it is wise to have a clear picture of what is wanted so that these goals can be met. Based on a company's track record there are no guarantees, but it is a nice assumption that those funds will remain consistent for the long term. It is good to become a long-term investor and it can be rewarding. The less you spend on a broker, the more that could be saved but for those with busy schedules brokers remain in the game. Some people only review things occasionally. I would recommend keeping an eye on things more cautiously with a broker regardless of what they records show. Not everything is predictable. Long-term investments are based on inflation so keep that in mind. If the inflation percentage is more than the rate in which the money is growing, you may end up with less. And while investing in mutual funds and stocks will continue to be based on market averages alone, it is a good place to be. Brokers are professionals and we can learn from the too. They know firsthand the affects of the market and how it may manipulate an individual stock in which actions are taken. That said, there is no right or wrong answer on whether or not an online investor should be used. It depends on the individual, the available amount of loot, and the expectations. Purchases in stock should be made over a period of time, not all at once. This way when prices are low or high reasonability is embraced. The stock market may seem anxious while media can sometimes seem negative, but things can be avoided. This includes fads and so forth where everyone does what others do. I hope I'm comfortable when I retire.

QUESTIONS TO ASK YOURSELF - INTERNALLY

1. How much money can you begin setting aside, big or small, for investing?

2. What is the difference between a 401(k) and a 403B?

3. What is the history of the stock market?

4. What are the benefits of short-term investing versus long-term investing?

5. What is a portfolio and what is its main goal?

6. What is the difference between a first time investor and a hard-core investor?

7. What do you want to buy when you retire?

8. How many kids are you planning on sending to college?

9. What are the minimum requirements in opening an investment account?

10. How are individual investments taxed?

11. What is the difference between an IRA and a ROTH IRA?

12. What is a margin?

13. What is inflation?

14. What are the signs of scammers?

15. What are the purposes of charts?

16. What are the main differences between stocks, bonds, mutual funds, IRAs, CDs, etc?

17. What is an IPO?

18. How many reasons do you have to invest?

19. How soon would you need the money?

20. How much can you afford to lose?

21. What is a good return on an investment?

22. How much time can you commit to your investments versus a broker?

23. How much does your employer have to offer when it comes to your future?

24. Who is Edgar?

REMINDERS

1. Go with what you know

2. Consider your time

3. Do the Research

4. Learn the Lingo

5. Trust you Instincts

Visit **www.goodmoney.com**

Author Biography

Michelle Hooper has worked as a commercial real estate reporter for a publishing company in Northern California. She observed investment strategies, trends in the mortgage market, and REIT investments making observations on mortgages and other financing when deemed necessary. Reviews on investment returns and the most popular markets for investors in the real estate world were noted. She has completed real estate and financial classes aside from her college degree in Mass Communications and Public Relations. Additionally, she has obtained her California real estate license. She works in Public Relations for Wolf Communications in Santa Rosa, California in addition to Century 21. If there is any spare time to be had, she loves to freelance write. Santa Rosa is her place of residence. She is an investor.

Index